Medieval Land Reclamation at Brayford Pool, Lincoln

Archaeological excavation at
the Brayford Centre
2000

Simon Carlyle
Rob Atkins

with contributions from

John Carrott, Margaret J. Darling, Karen Deighton,
Rowena Gale, John Giorgi, Alison Locker, Michelle Morris,
James Rackham, David Smith and Jane Young

Illustrations by

Jacqueline Harding
Pat Walsh

BAR British Series 498
2009

Published in 2016 by
BAR Publishing, Oxford

BAR British Series 498

Medieval Land Reclamation at Brayford Pool, Lincoln

ISBN 978 1 4073 0602 5

BAR Publishing is the trading name of British Archaeological Reports (Oxford) Ltd.
British Archaeological Reports was first incorporated in 1974 to publish the BAR
Series, International and British. In 1992 Hadrian Books Ltd became part of the BAR
group. This volume was originally published by Archaeopress in conjunction with
British Archaeological Reports (Oxford) Ltd / Hadrian Books Ltd, the Series principal
publisher, in 2009. This present volume is published by BAR Publishing, 2016.

Printed in England

BAR
PUBLISHING

BAR titles are available from:

    BAR Publishing
    122 Banbury Rd, Oxford, OX2 7BP, UK
EMAIL   info@barpublishing.com
PHONE   +44 (0)1865 310431
FAX   +44 (0)1865 316916
    www.barpublishing.com

Contents

		Page
Contributors		vii
Acknowledgements		viii
Summary		ix

Chapter 1: Introduction — 1

Background	1
Topography and geology	1
Historical and archaeological background	1

Chapter 2: The Excavation Evidence — 5

Methodology	5
Pre-medieval deposits	5
Medieval, phase 1: Initial land reclamation (later 11th century)	7
Medieval, phase 2: Early pits and boundary ditches (late 11th to mid 12th centuries)	7
Medieval, phase 3: Further pits and a boundary ditch (late 11th to mid 12th centuries)	10
Medieval, phase 4: An organic soil horizon (late 11th to mid 12th centuries)	10
Medieval, phase 5: Possible timber buildings and associated pits (mid 12th century)	10
Medieval, phase 6: Timber slot, ditch and cobble spread (mid 12th century)	13
Medieval, phase 7: Land reclamation (late 12th century)	17
Medieval, phase 8: Dark soil horizon (later medieval)	19
Modern deposits	19

Chapter 3: The Finds — 20

The Roman pottery *by Margaret J Darling*	20
The medieval pottery *by Jane Young*	20
The ceramic building material *by Jane Young*	21
The non-ceramic finds *by Tora Hylton*	21
The leather *by June Swann*	22

Chapter 4: Environmental Evidence — 23

Introduction *by James Rackham*	23
Core samples *by James Rackham*	23
The natural sedimentary sequence	23
Plant remains *by John Giorgi*	25
Insect remains *by David Smith and Michelle Morris*	41
Charcoal and waterlogged wood *by Rowena Gale*	47
Parasite eggs *by John Carrot*	51
Fish bones *by Alison Locker*	58
Animal bones *by Karen Deighton*	59

Marine shells *by James Rackham*   60

Freshwater and terrestrial molluscs *by James Rackham*   60

Overview and interpretation of the deposits *by James Rackham*   61

Chapter 5: General Discussion   70

Prehistoric and Roman deposits   70

Medieval occupation   70

Bibliography   74

Figures

Page

1: Site location plan   2

2: Trench location plan   3

3: East-facing section of trench   6

4: Phase 1, land surface (late 11th century)   8

5: Phase 2, early pits and boundary ditches (late 11th to mid 12th centuries)   9

6: Phase 3, ditches and pits (late 11th to mid 12th centuries)   11

7: Phase 4, soil development (late 11th to mid 12th centuries)   12

8: Phase 5, timber building and pits (mid 12th century)   14

9: Phase 6, timber slot, ditch and cobble spread (mid 12th century)   15

10: Phase 7, land reclamation (late 12th century)   16

11: A large medieval jar, layer 210   17

12: Phase 8, later medieval soil horizon   18

13: The total number of individuals and species for the insect faunas   41

14: The proportions of ecological groupings in the samples   42

15: The proportions of synanthropic groupings in the samples   42

16: Plotted trichurid egg measurements with overlay of size ranges for eggs of trichurids of several common   53
     domesticated animals and *Trichuris trichiura*

17: Plotted *Trichuris* measurements by sample   54

18: Plotted trichurid egg measurements with overlay of size ranges for eggs of *Trichuris trichiura* and *T. suis*   55

19a: Histograms of the distributions of polar plug to polar plug maximum length and maximum width   57
     measurements (samples 9 and 11)

19b: Histograms of the distributions of polar plug to polar plug maximum length (samples 12 and 3)   58

19c: Histograms of the distributions of polar plug to polar plug maximum width (samples 12 and 3)   58

19d: Histograms of the distributions of polar plug to polar plug maximum length and width (all samples)   58

20: Brayford Pool and the City of Lincoln   71

Plates

1: General view of the site from the adjacent multi-storey car park, facing east   1

2: General view of the trench, facing north   5

3: Pit 144, facing west   13

4: Slot 140, facing south   13

5: Cobble spread, facing north   17

6: Wooden stakes (213) in west-facing section   17

Tables

Page

1: Suggested deposition date of stratified pottery groups from contexts ... 20

2: Pottery codenames and total quantities by sherd, weight (g) and vessel count ... 21

3: Summary of tile by context ... 21

4: Finds from the environmental samples ... 24

5a: Environmental finds from the samples ... 25

5b: Environmental finds from the samples ... 26

6: The plant remains from Phases 1, 2 and 3 ... 33

7: The plant remains from Phases 2, 3, 4 and 5a ... 36

8: The plant remains from Phases 5b and 6 ... 38

9: The insect remains ... 44

10: The proportion of ecological groupings present in the samples ... 46

11: The proportions of synanthropic groupings present in the samples ... 46

12: The total numbers of individuals and species for the insect faunas ... 46

13: Charcoal and waterlogged wood from Phases 2, 3, 5 and 6 ... 50

14: Measurements for trichurid eggs in microns ... 52

15: Descriptive statistics for polar plug to polar plug maximum length (l) and maximum width (w) measurements by sample ... 56

16: Measurements of unfertilised *Ascaris* eggs from all samples ... 57

17: Fish bones recovered from the soil samples ... 59

18: Animal species present by anatomical element ... 60

19: Birds by context ... 60

20: Ribs and vertebrae ... 60

21: Frequency of valves or shells of hand collected marine molluscs and garden snails ... 61

22: Freshwater and terrestrial snails identified ... 61

23: Summary of material in each sample taken from post-excavation analysis and assessment data ... 62

24: Frequency of samples in which each identified food taxa was recorded ... 66

25: Frequency of samples with seeds of plants with medicinal qualities ... 68

Contributors

Simon Carlyle BSc, MSc, MIfA
Senior Project Officer, Northamptonshire Archaeology, 2 Bolton House, Wootton Hall Park, Northampton NN4 8BE

Rob Atkins BSocSc, DipArch
Project Officer, Oxford East, 15 Trafalgar Way, Bar Hill, Cambridgeshire CB23 8SQ

Margaret J Darling Mphil, FSA, MIfA
Archaeological Consultant, 25 West Parade, Lincoln LN1 1NW

Jane Young
Archaeological Consultant, 25 West Parade, Lincoln LN1 1NW

Tora Hylton
Finds Project Officer, Northamptonshire Archaeology

D James Rackham BSc, MSc, FSA
The Environmental Archaeology Consultancy, Chantry Cottage, 25 Main Street, South Rauceby, Lincolnshire NG34 8QG

John A Giorgi
Puddavine Terrace, Dartington, Totnes, Devon

David Smith MA Cantab, MA Sheffield, PhD
Institute of Archaeology and Antiquity, University of Birmingham

Michelle Morris BA, MA
Institute of Archaeology and Antiquity, University of Birmingham

John Carrott
Palaeoecology Research Services, Unit 8, Dabble Duck Industrial Estate, Shildon, County Durham DL4 2RA

Alison Locker BSc, PhD
L'Ensoleillée, 20 Bld de Garavan, 06500 Menton, France

Rowena Gale
Honorary Research Associate, Royal Botanic Gardens, Kew

Karen Deighton MSc
Environmental Project Officer, Northamptonshire Archaeology

June Swann MBE
Retired: Former Keeper of the Boot and Shoe Collection, Central Museum and Art Gallery, Northampton and International Consultant on the History of Shoes and Shoemaking

Acknowledgements

Northamptonshire Archaeology is grateful to Simons Estates for funding the archaeological work. The work was undertaken through John Samuels Archaeological Consultants, the mitigation strategy and fieldwork management being undertaken by Nansi Rosenberg. Michael Jones the City of Lincoln Archaeologist monitored the work and gave valuable advice on the archaeological background to the area of the city. Palaeo-environmental consultancy was provided by James Rackham.

The project was managed for Northamptonshire Archaeology by Andrew Mudd and the fieldwork directed by Rob Atkins with the assistance of Erlend Hindmarch, Ian Fisher, Karen Deighton and Simon Carlyle. Following post-excavation assessment, Simon Carlyle collated the various strands of analysis and produced this synthesised report. Illustrations are by Jacqueline Harding and Pat Walsh of Northamptonshire Archaeology. Editing for publication is by Andy Chapman and Pat Chapman. Typeset and page design by Past Historic, Kings Stanley, Gloucestershire, GL10 3HW

The archive of finds and archaeological records from this project are to be housed with the City and County Museum, Lincoln, under Accession Code 2000.62.

Summary

In June 2000, a small excavation was carried out by Northamptonshire Archaeology on land on the north bank of Brayford Pool, Lincoln, in the area of medieval Baxtergate. The earliest horizons were identified in two cores taken from deposits in the base of the trench. Environmental analysis of the cores, assisted by two radiocarbon dates, showed that peat began to accumulate along the Pool margins in the late Bronze Age, probably developing into a fen carr type habitat. A change from woody to fibrous peat in the late prehistoric or Roman period implies a significant change in the local environment, possibly associated with the use of the foreshore as a 'hard' to serve the Roman military and then the colonia in the 1st century AD. Peat continued to accumulate until around the late 7th century AD, when the ground appears to have dried out sufficiently to encourage marginal settlement in the area.

Within the trench, archaeological remains, broadly dating to the 11th and 12th centuries AD, were found beneath a thick layer of modern demolition rubble. The medieval remains comprised features typical of 'backyard' activity, such as cess and general refuse pits, and ditches and gullies which probably functioned as plot boundaries and drains. The tentative remains of a partitioned timber building, possibly used as a latrine and/or an animal byre, were also found. This activity was interspersed with a series of layers, probably associated with attempts to reclaim land along the northern edge of Brayford Pool or placed to protect the bank of the Pool from erosion. Environmental evidence was used to characterize the medieval deposits in order to assist in determining the function of the features, as well as providing information about the local environment at this time. Later medieval and post-medieval horizons had been totally destroyed by 19th and 20th-century development.

Chapter 1: Introduction

Background

In June 2000 a small excavation was carried out on a plot of land on the north bank of Brayford Pool, Lincoln (site centred on NGR SK 7125 9729; Fig 1, Plate 1). The land was subject to plans for commercial redevelopment by Simons Estates, the new development including a multi-screen cinema and retail units. The excavation formed part of a scheme of archaeological investigation, managed by John Samuels Archaeological Consultants (JSAC), comprising a desk-based assessment, a test-pit evaluation, an excavation and a watching brief. The archaeological work was carried out on behalf of Simons Estates to a specification prepared by JSAC (Samuels and Rosenberg 2000). The excavation was undertaken by Northamptonshire Archaeology and forms the subject of this report.

In order to preserve surviving archaeological remains on the site *in situ*, with minimum disturbance or destruction, a decision was made to support the foundations of the new buildings on *c* 800 concrete piles, each 10m long, driven into the soft ground. However, negotiations between JSAC, the developers, and the City of Lincoln Archaeologist, Michael Jones, led to the decision to excavate an area where the density of the piles could not adequately ensure the survival of archaeological deposits.

The excavation took place in the eastern half of the site, just to the north of two trenches excavated in 1975 that produced evidence associated with the late medieval and post-medieval waterfront (Fig 2; Jones and Jones 1981; Steane *et al* 2001). At the surface the excavation trench measured 19m by 4.5m. Its location was kindly plotted by surveyors from Simons Estates and was opened up under archaeological control using their machinery.

Topography and geology

The site covered an area of *c* 0.5ha to the south of Lincoln city centre, approximately 0.6km from the cathedral and just within the medieval walled town. The excavation trench was 51m from the northern edge of Brayford Pool, at *c* 5m OD, on land gradually sloping down towards the Pool. The underlying geology has been classified as undifferentiated alluvium overlying Lias Clay (Robson *et al* 1974).

Historical and archaeological background

Lincoln was founded in the later 1st century AD as a Roman *colonia*, following a period of Roman military occupation in the area. Excavations around Lincoln show that the town expanded rapidly from the 10th to the 12th centuries, with suburbs developing to the north, north-east, west, east and south of the walled city (Vince 1993, 165). Since the medieval period the area has been called Newland, reflecting land reclamation on the northern margins of the Brayford Pool, although it was originally probably referred to as *Baxtergate*; the medieval suburb of *Newland* lay immediately to the west, beyond the city wall.

Plate 1: General view of the site from the adjacent multi-storey car park, facing east

1

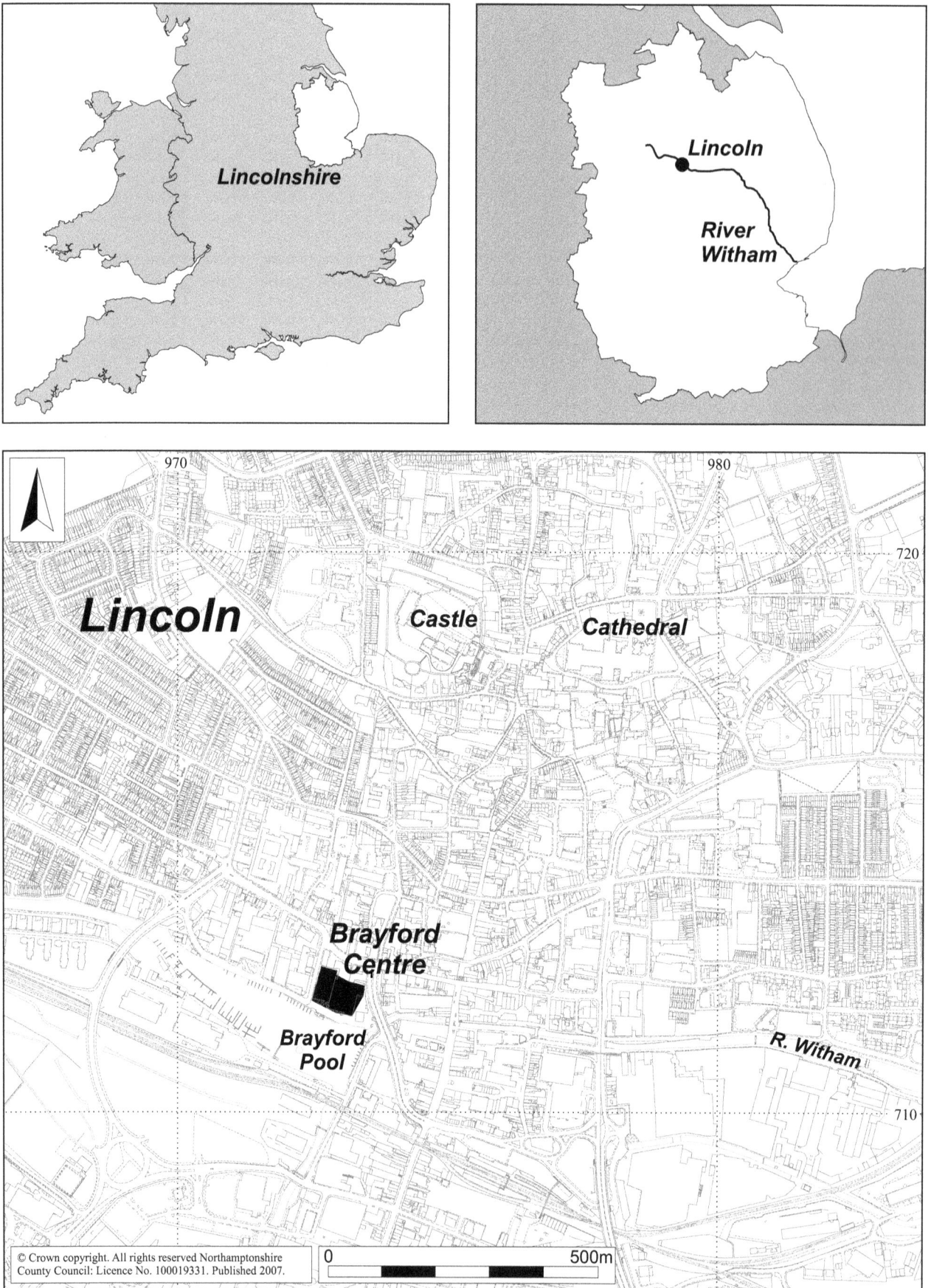

Fig 1: Site location plan

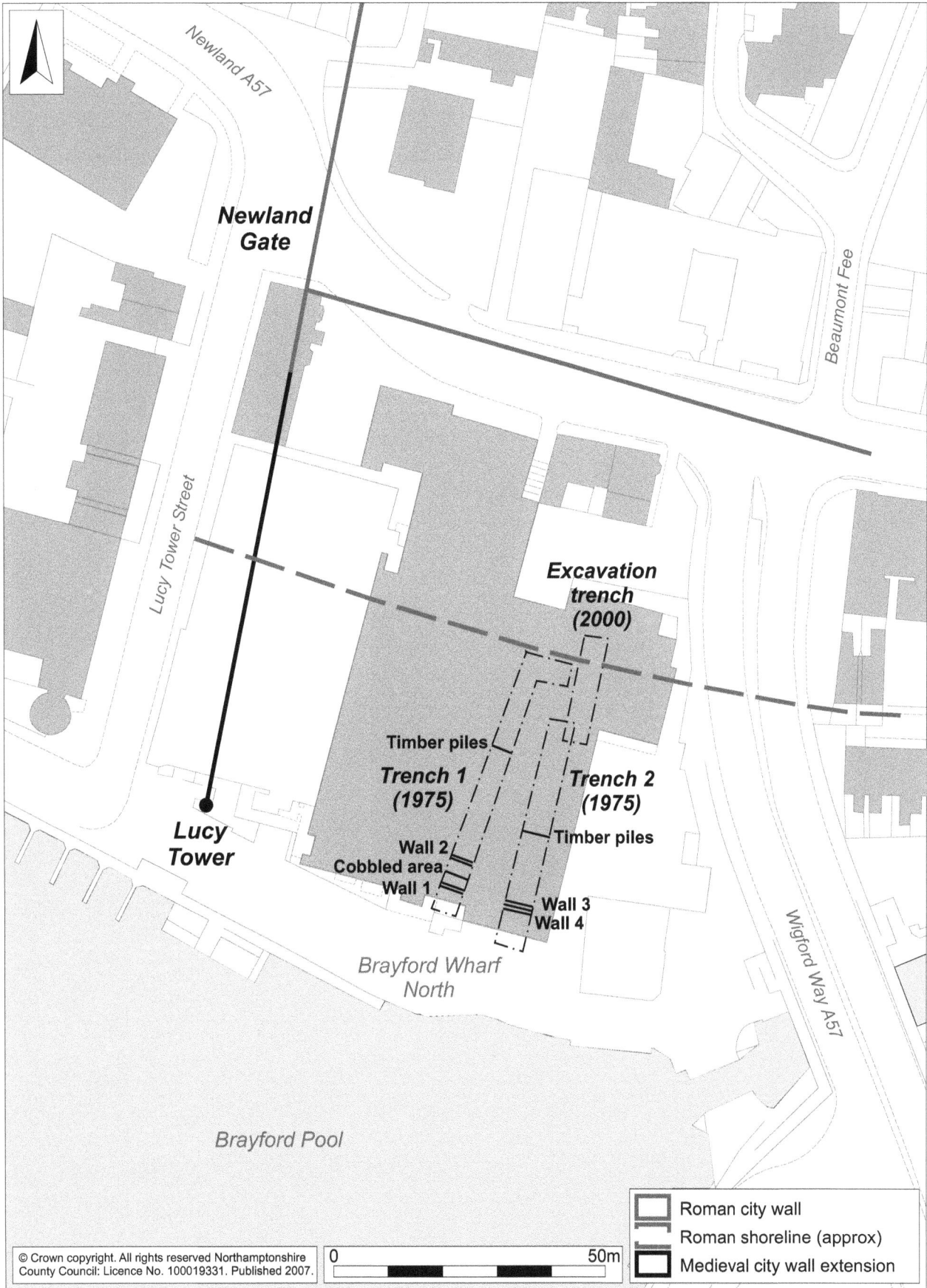

Fig 2: Trench location plan

Previously, there have been three trenches excavated within the development area. The first of these was excavated in 1972 on the site of the medieval Lucy tower, and in 1975 two trenches were excavated in the south-east quarter of the site (Fig 2; Colyer 1975; Jones and Jones 1981; Steane *et al* 2001). The excavated evidence indicated that the site lay just to the south of the Roman *colonia*, the southern perimeter of which probably followed the line of Newland, the modern street that forms the northern edge of the development area.

In the earlier excavation, located on the site of the Lucy Tower, evidence was found for land reclamation along the north bank of Brayford Pool in the medieval period. The tower, which was built in the late 13th or early 14th century at the southern end of an extension to the city wall, was constructed on a raft of grass, twigs, reeds and other vegetation. Well-preserved organic material, including leather and wood, was found in the ditch next to the tower. An earlier ditch, probably the continuation of the Roman city ditch, was found to run on approximately the same alignment down to the margins of Brayford Pool (Colyer 1975, 264; Steane *et al* 2001, 136-151).

The two trenches opened up in 1975 were excavated in less than ideal conditions, ahead of the construction of a supermarket (Jones and Jones 1981; Steane *et al* 2001). Archaeological remains, which have been interpreted as successive phases of waterfront walls and buildings, were found. The remains consisted of rows of timber piles and stone walls running parallel to the north bank of the Pool, a cobbled area and clay floors. The phasing and dating of the remains was never elucidated. They were thought to date from the late medieval period, but the present work suggests they could have originated in the 11th century and run through to the 14th century. Later in the same year, two test pits were excavated in the north-east and north-west corners of the site and revealed at least *c* 5m of undated loam and silt deposits, lying beneath 19th-century occupation levels. Some of these deposits may relate to the reclamation of land in the medieval period, overlying earlier Roman and prehistoric horizons.

Chapter 2: The excavated evidence

Methodology

The trench was excavated using a JCB-type mechanical excavator, fitted with a toothless ditching blade. The trench was aligned from north to south and at the surface (*c* 5m OD) measured 19m long by 4.5m wide (Plate 2). Due to the depth of the excavation and the unconsolidated debris overlying the archaeological remains the trench was stepped, with the base of the trench (*c* 3m OD) measuring 14.2m long and 1.9m wide. Mechanical excavation was carried out under archaeological supervision and proceeded to the top of significant archaeological deposits. All subsequent cleaning and excavation was undertaken by hand, with the exception of the mechanical excavation of two sondages at either end of the trench.

The medieval deposits, which broadly date to the 11th and 12th centuries, have been assigned to eight phases (Phases 1-8). They are preceded by prehistoric through to Late Saxon deposits identified in two boreholes sunk in the base of the trench, and are sealed by modern demolition deposits. Due to the relatively short period of time spanned by Phases 1-8 and the lack of tight chronological definition obtainable from the dating evidence, the phasing is based largely on stratigraphical relationships and the grouping of features associated with episodes of occupational activity and land reclamation. Although there is a slight trend in the dating of the pottery between the earlier and later phases, precise dating of these phases is not achievable. Later medieval and post-medieval deposits had been truncated by modern development, and modern demolition rubble directly overlay the 11th to 12th-century medieval remains.

The sequence can be summarised as follows:

Plate 2: General view of the trench, facing north

Pre-medieval deposits

Boreholes were sunk at either end of the trench (BH1 and BH2). The cores extracted from the boreholes are

Period	Phase	Description
Pre-Bronze Age		Lacustrine silts
Bronze Age - Saxon		Woody peat with organic sands
Later Saxon		Drying out of peat deposits
Medieval (later 11th century)	1	Initial land reclamation
Medieval (late 11th to mid 12th centuries)	2	Settlement waste, early pits and boundary ditches
Medieval (late 11th to mid 12th centuries)	3	Settlement waste, pits and boundary ditch
Medieval (late 11th to mid 12th centuries)	4	Organic soil horizon
Medieval (mid 12th century)	5	Possible timber buildings and pits
Medieval (mid 12th century)	6	Possible timber building and cobble surface
Medieval (late 12th century)	7	Fence line, settlement waste
Later medieval?	8	Dark soil horizon
Modern		Truncation deposits

Section 1 - East facing

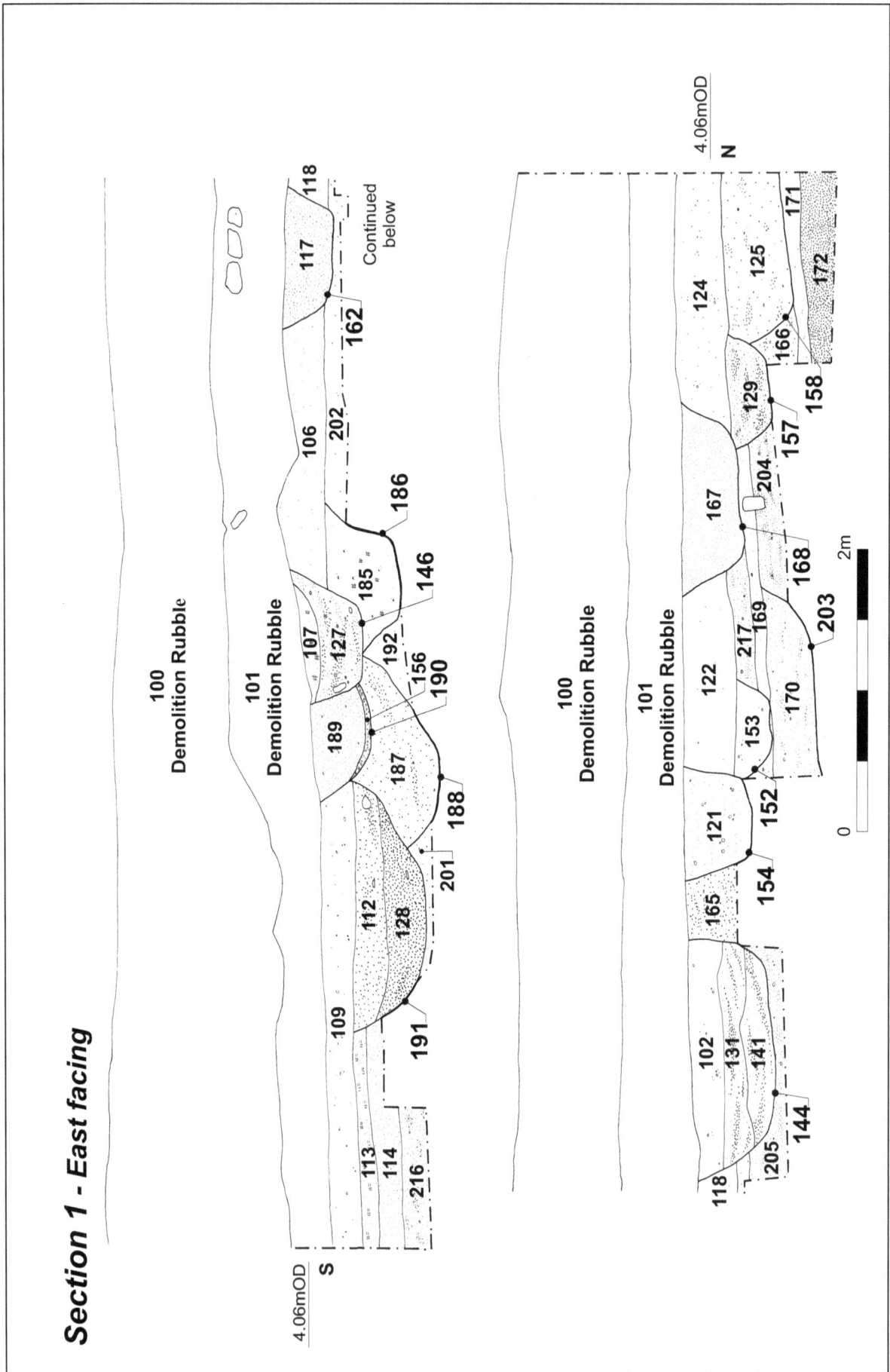

Fig 3: East-facing section of trench

reported on in detail below (Rackham, this report) and only a summary of the findings is given here.

The earliest deposits consist of fine to medium grey sands, containing some organic material in the form of organic silts and wood fragments. These sands are alluvial in origin and form part of a suite of undifferentiated alluvial sands and gravels that overlie the Lias clay of the valley floor. In BH2 the sands are overlain by a thin layer of laminated organic silts, probably lacustrine in origin, deposited in the slow moving waters of Brayford Pool.

In the late Bronze Age a thick woody peat bed began to accumulate, interleaved with organic sands derived from slope wash close to the Pool margins. Lenses of sand in the upper peat horizons could derive from local ground disturbance associated with Roman and Saxon activity along the north bank of Brayford Pool or from major flooding episodes. Peat formation continued until the Saxon period (AD 660-900), when changes in water levels led to the partial desiccation of deposits at the Pool edge, possibly encouraging more permanent settlement in the vicinity in the late Saxon period.

Medieval, phase 1: Initial land reclamation (later 11th century)

Phase 1 deposits comprised a succession of layers, recorded intermittently in section along the full length of the trench and in the base of the sondages (Figs 3 and 4). Later features cut these layers.

Probably the earliest deposit in the sequence, layer 172, was exposed in the base of the sondage at the northern end of the trench (c 3.3m OD). It consisted of orange-brown peaty sand and yielded mid to late 11th-century pottery sherds, in addition to residual Roman tile fragments, including a large piece of tegula. The presence of the residual Roman material, freshwater faunal remains and the high sand and gravel component of the deposit suggests that this layer is largely colluvial in origin, and formed from slope wash combined with organic material accumulated on the margins of the Pool. Numerous rootlets in this layer imply a vegetated surface and it therefore probably represents the original land surface prior to land reclamation at the Pool edge in the late 11th to 12th centuries. Insect and weed evidence indicates occasional deposition of some settlement waste along the Pool margins, although the environmental evidence is generally typical of a marginal aquatic environment, subject to seasonal flooding.

The remaining layers fall into two main categories. The first category contains those layers that were either brown, red-brown or grey organic silts (166, 171, 192, 201, and 202); the second comprises layers of dirty yellow sands (114, 204, 205 and 216). Given the short period of time between the formation of the basal layer 172 and subsequent archaeological activity, these layers probably represent deliberate deposition to stabilise and build up ground level on the north bank of Brayford Pool. This was probably done haphazardly over a period of time rather than as a single event, and may reflect increasing settlement along the Pool margins. It is likely that the organic silts derive from dumps of soil and organic material, including some settlement waste, and the dirty

sands from redeposited alluvial and terrestrial sands. These layers were conspicuous for their lack of dating evidence; the only artefact found was a residual sherd of Roman brick from layer 166.

The only layer not mentioned so far is layer 113, the latest in the sequence of layers at the southern end of the trench. It differed from the deposits described above, in that it was grey clayey sand and contained eight sherds of mid/late 11th to mid 12th-century pottery and 25 fragments of animal bone. This layer provides the earliest clear indication of settlement in the immediate vicinity at this period of time.

Medieval, phase 2: Early pits and boundary ditches (late 11th to mid 12th centuries)

Following the initial build-up of the ground surface along the Pool margins, the earliest activity revealed in the trench, other than the disposal of settlement waste, was the cutting of three pits and two ditches, sometime in the late 11th to mid 12th centuries (Figs 3 and 5).

Pit 203, which was roughly aligned from north-east to south-west, was broad and shallow (0.32m deep) with a flat base. Only the base and the short, steep northern edge of the pit were exposed; its full dimensions could not be determined. The fill (170) of the pit had a relatively low organic content and a high gravel content, suggesting that it may have been deliberately backfilled with re-deposited alluvial sands and gravel shortly after it was excavated. At the northern end of the trench, pit 158 was similarly broad and shallow (0.46m deep), with a flat base and short, steep sides. It extended beyond the limits of the trench and only the south-east corner of the feature was revealed. The fill (125) of the pit, which contained sherds of pottery dating from the mid 11th to mid 12th centuries, produced a significant quantity of freshwater mollusc shells from species that inhabit large bodies of water, like the Pool. These species would not inhabit the foul, stagnant environment of a damp or water-filled pit or ditch and it seems likely that they were introduced to the pit by flooding or were included in the disposal in the pit of reeds cut from the Pool margins.

At the southern end of the trench a large oval pit (134), which was only observed in plan, was largely truncated by two ditches. The ditches (186 and 188) were parallel and adjacent, and it is likely that they are sequential, possibly defining the southern boundary of a settlement plot. Running from east to west, they were on the same alignment as the walls and timber revetments revealed in the trenches excavated in 1975. Ditch 186 was at least 1.05m wide, 0.54m deep and had relatively steep sides and a flat base; ditch 188 had a rather irregular concave profile, was at least 1.3m wide and had a depth of 0.64m. The relationship between the two ditches, which both produced pottery sherds broadly dating from the 11th to the late 12th centuries, could not be determined due to truncation by later activity. In ditch 188, which appears to have silted up gradually over a period of time, the environment supported an insect fauna indicative of foul rotting matter, dung and cess.

Although there were variations in the organic and mineral component of the fills in the above features, they all

Upper Excavated Surface

166

113

114

Lower Excavated Surface

172

204

205

114

216

S.1

S.1

Phase 1

Piles

0

5m

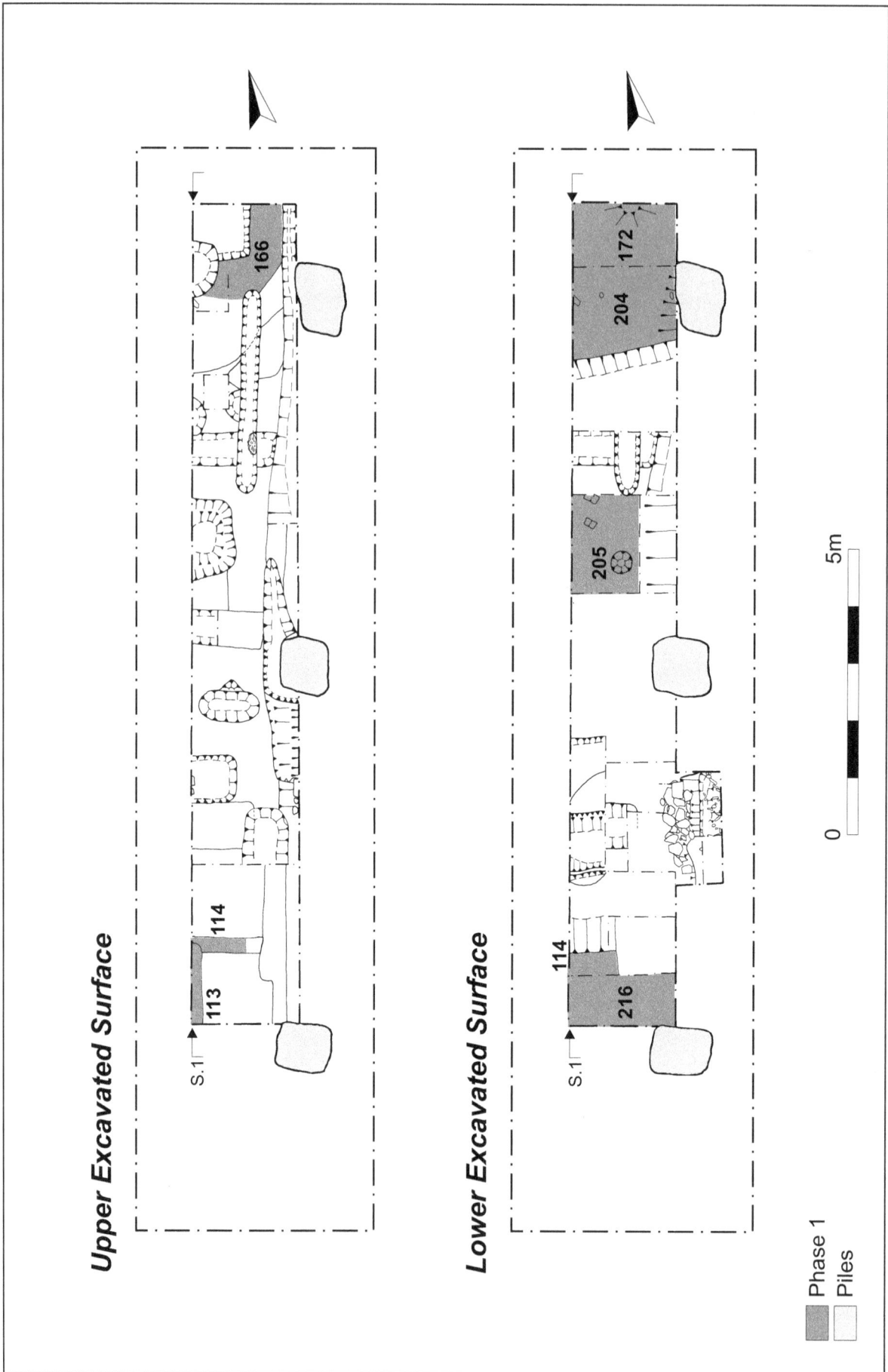

Fig 4: Phase 1, land surface (late 11th century)

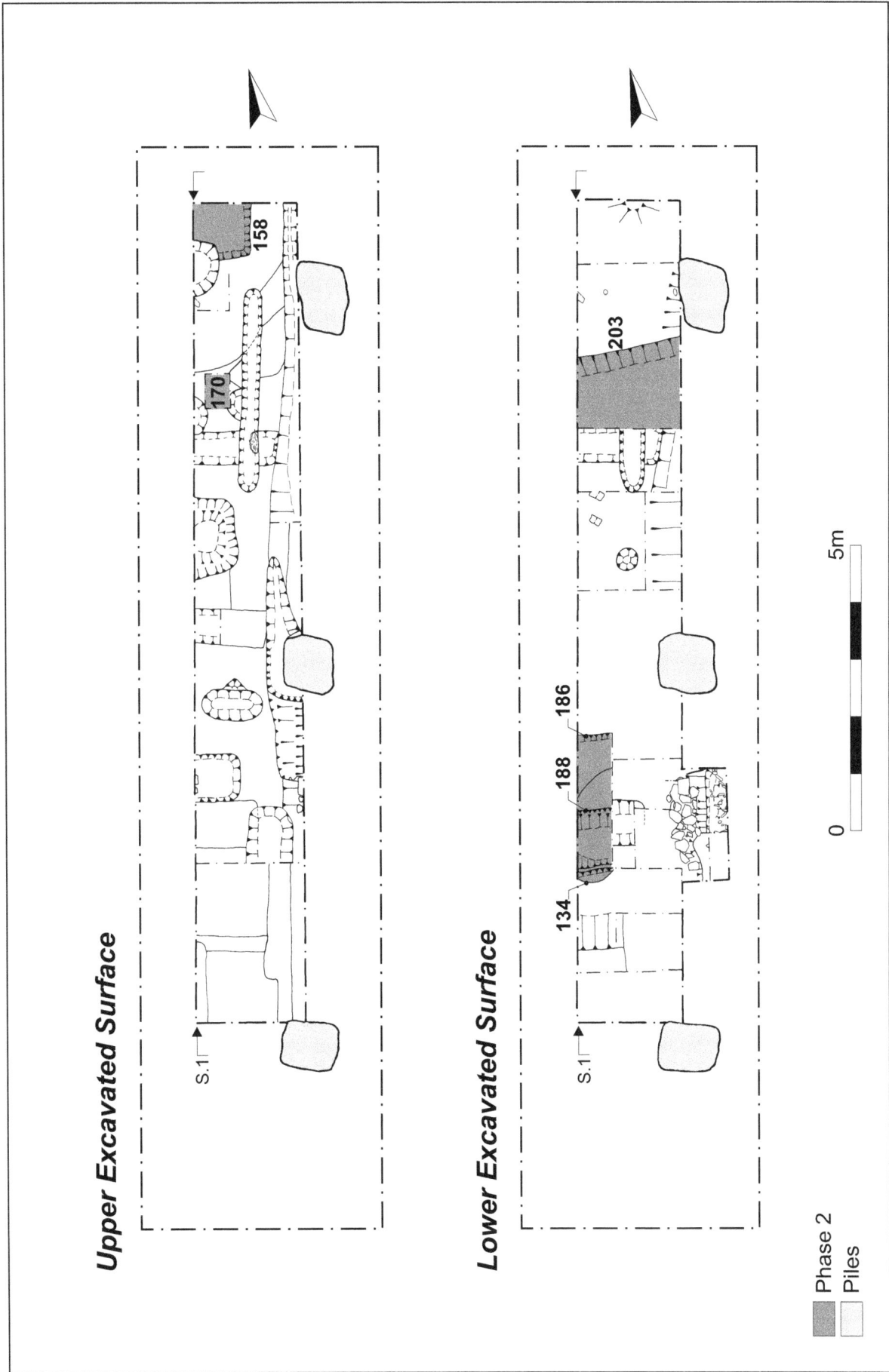

Upper Excavated Surface

158

170

S.1

Lower Excavated Surface

203

186

188

134

S.1

Phase 2

Piles

0   5m

Fig 5: Phase 2, early pits and boundary ditches (late 11th to mid 12th centuries)

displayed evidence for a wet, aquatic, open environment along the north bank of Brayford Pool at this time. The shore, which was probably still subject to seasonal flooding, was colonised by wetland plants and supported a fauna of aquatic insects and molluscs. The remains of freshwater snails and *Daphnia* (waterflea) ephippia were found in most fills.

Medieval, phase 3: Further pits and a boundary ditch (late 11th to mid 12th centuries)

Once the Phase 2 ditches and pits had been back-filled or silted up, renewed activity is evident on the site, consisting of a sequence of thin layers across the northern half of the trench, the cutting of a large ditch that ran parallel and adjacent to the Phase 2 ditches, and several pits (Figs 3 and 6).

Extending across the northern end of the trench, in a broad band *c* 3m wide, there was a sequence of three thin layers (169, 217 and 126) deposited over the area of pit 203 (Phase 2). These layers had a combined thickness of *c* 0.20m and consisted of either dark sandy silt or relatively clean sand. They may have been deposited in order to level a hollow in the ground in this area, or accumulated over time from material washed downslope into the hollow.

Roughly contemporary with these layers was a broad ditch (191), 1.75m wide and 0.51m deep, crossing the southern end of the trench on an east to west alignment. The ditch, which contained pottery sherds dated to the mid 11th to mid 12th centuries, appears to have been cut as a reaffirmation of the probable boundary described by the two Phase 2 ditches. The fills of this ditch (128 and 112) also contained significant concentrations of cess, suggesting that the ditch may have also served as the outflow of a latrine or as a convenient place to dispose of human faecal waste. The inclusion of cess was indicated by the presence of cereal bran, apple endocarp fragments and flax seeds, in addition to the ova of parasitic intestinal worms. Such worms can also infest pigs, and the identification of likely straw fragments in the ditch deposits may indicate that straw bedding, mixed with pig dung, was also discarded in the ditch. However, the straw may also derive from discarded floor covering and bedding associated with human habitation. Moss, which was also found in these deposits, and indeed straw, may have been used for sanitary hygiene purposes.

On the eastern side of the trench ditch 191 was cut by a large pit (193), which extended beyond the limits of the trench. The pit, which had almost vertical sides and was only partially excavated, was over 1.1m wide, 1.8m long and 0.45m deep. Two sherds of a small jar or pitcher, broadly dated to the 11th to 12th centuries, were recovered from its fill (194).

In the northern half of the trench two pits (152 and 157) cut layer 217. Pit 152, which had short, steep-sloping sides and a flat base, was approximately 0.7m wide and had a depth of 0.24m. Faunal remains in the fill (153), including water flea ephippia, freshwater snail shells and caddis larval cases, indicate the continuance of wet conditions along the north bank of the Pool, at least on a seasonal basis.

Pit 157, which was *c* 0.8m wide and 0.28m deep, had

a similar profile to pit 152. The fill (129) contained some elements indicative of cess, with the exception of cereal bran and apple endocarp fragments, which were absent. There was also a lower count of cess-related insect remains and parasitic ova were absent. The pit therefore probably functioned as a general refuse pit, an interpretation supported by the inclusion in the fill of 11th to mid 12th-century pottery sherds and a fragment of leather.

Medieval, phase 4: An organic soil horizon (late 11th to mid 12th centuries)

Extending in section along the full length of the trench there was a layer of dark grey-brown compact, organic silt (106, 109, 111, 115, 118, 122, 124 and 165) (Figs 3 and 7). The deposit was up to 0.35m thick, sealed all earlier phases of activity and was cut by later features. It is possible that the upper part of the layer and later features cut into it had been truncated by modern activity.

The organic component was highly degraded, indicative of a biologically-active soil horizon, and the presence of plant rootlets suggests that vegetation was established on the surface of the deposit. A small concentration of pottery sherds was recovered from deposit 106, near the centre of the trench, indicating a late 11th to mid 12th-century date for the formation of the deposit. Fragments of animal bone and a small whetstone were also recovered from this layer. The plant remains identified from a sample taken from 106 were restricted to weeds of disturbed and waste ground, and provided little evidence for human settlement or activity in the area at this time. It is likely, however, that settlement was continuous in the immediate vicinity throughout the medieval period, and that the absence or reduction in environmental evidence for human habitation is related to local changes in land use.

Medieval, phase 5: Possible timber buildings and associated pits (mid 12th century)

Sub-phase 5a, the possible timber building

This sub-phase represents the earliest features cut into the Phase 4 ground surface (Figs 3 and 8). These were four sub-rectangular pits or slot terminals (154, 162, 168 and 190), that continued beyond the limits of the trench to the west. They were approximately 0.8m to 1.2m wide, 0.34m to 0.48m deep, and had short, steeply sloping sides and flat bases. These features appear to have been cut at roughly the same time as they were of a similar size and profile, ran parallel with each other and terminated in a line at the same point. They were spaced between 1.2m and 2.2m apart.

The purpose of these features is uncertain and their clean, sandy fills contained limited environmental evidence to cast light on their function. The southernmost pit/slot terminal (190) appeared to have a brushwood lining. It is possible that they served as the footings for a timber building constructed on timber ring beams and provided a firm foundation in an area of soft ground. The regularity of the slots supports this interpretation. A single sherd from the base of a jar, broadly dated to the mid 11th to mid 12th centuries, was found in slot terminal/pit 154.

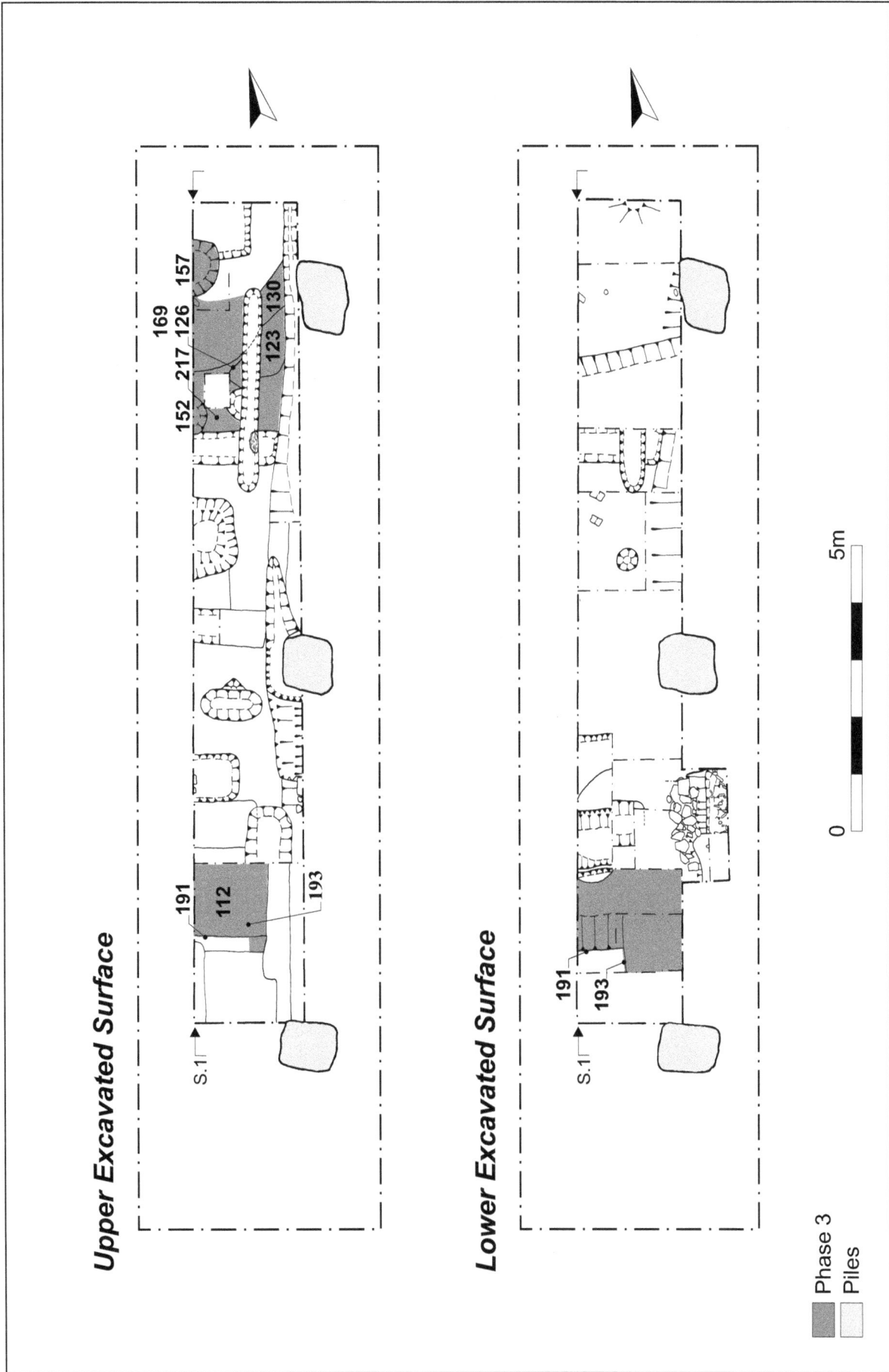

Fig 6: Phase 3, ditches and pits (late 11th to mid 12th centuries)

Upper Excavated Surface

S.1

115

111

106

118

165

S.1

Lower Excavated Surface

165

5m

0

Phase 4

Piles

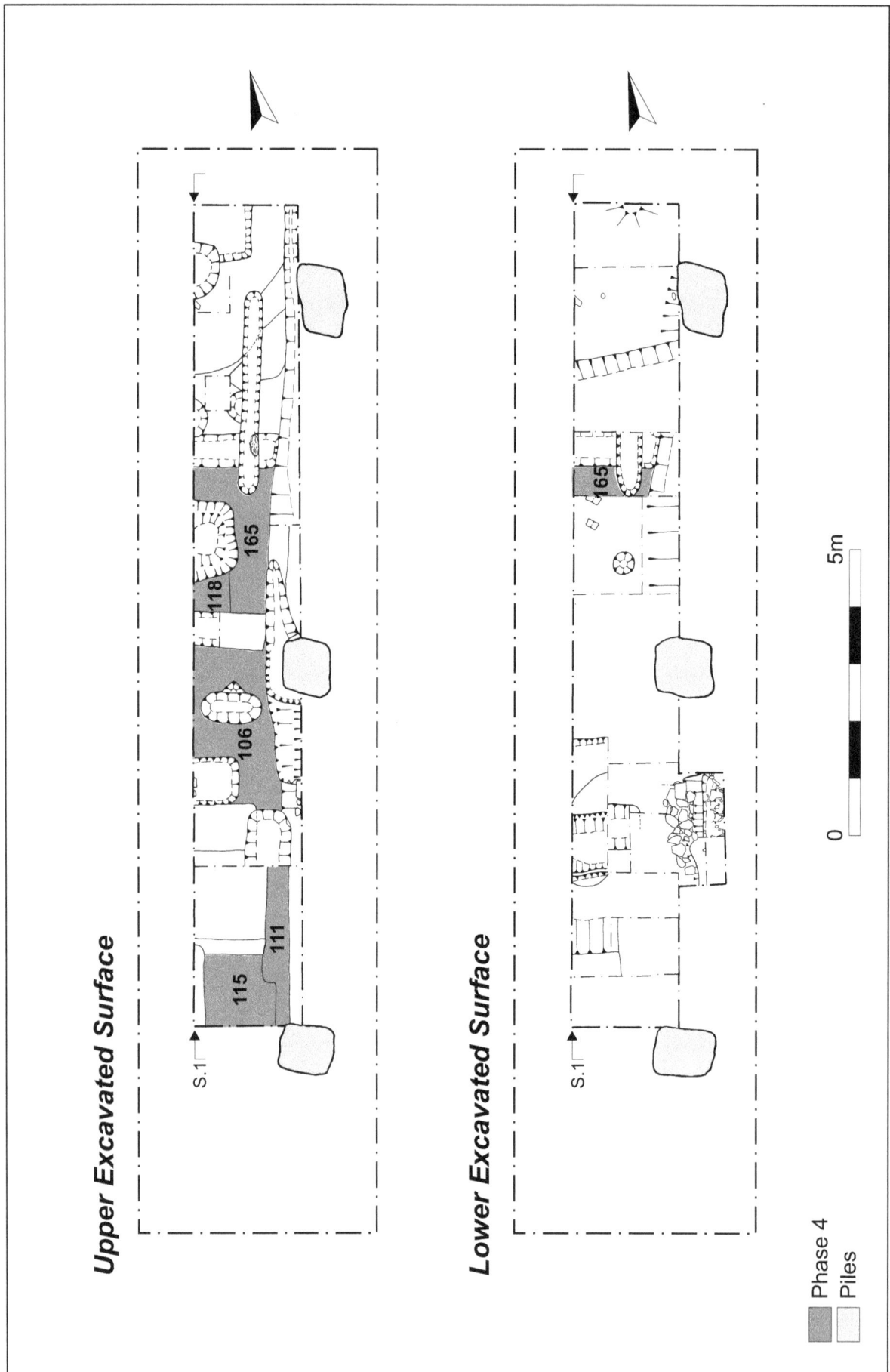

Fig 7: Phase 4, soil development (late 11th to mid 12th centuries)

Sub-phase 5b, domestic refuse pits and latrine pit

Lying between the sub-rectangular slots mentioned above (sub-phase 5a), and possibly internal to the suggested building, there were a number of pits of varying sizes.

The largest of the pits, pit 144, which was approximately 1.7m wide and 0.59m deep, was sub-rectangular and had steep, concave sides and a roughly flat base (Plate 3). It continued to the west beyond the limits of the trench. It contained fills (141, 131 and 102) and produced a small assemblage of pottery (10 sherds) dated to the 11th to 12th centuries (Fig 3). The deposits in the pit were strongly characteristic of sewage and the pit probably functioned as a cesspit or latrine.

Plate 3: Pit 144, facing west

Plate 4: Slot 140, facing south

The northern edge of the sub-rectangular pit/slot 190 was cut by a similar sub-rectangular feature (146). This feature measured 0.94m wide, 0.44m deep and continued beyond the limits of the trench to the west. Although similar in size and shape to the earlier feature, it differed considerably in terms of its fills (127 and 107), which consisted of a thin ashy layer over a dark brown organic silty sand (Fig 3). The primary fill 127 contained 72 animal bone fragments, representing approximately one fifth of the total animal bone assemblage from the site. At least seven different species were identified, including fish. Some of the bone was burnt and the presence in both fills of wood ash and charred and uncharred heather shoots, which were probably used as fuel, suggests that the pit was used primarily for the disposal of domestic waste, including cooking waste.

There were three other pits associated with this sub-phase of activity. Truncating pit 138, there was an oval pit (139) 1.1m long, 0.65m wide and 0.22m deep. The fill (105) was very similar in character and content to the fill of pit/ slot 146. The two remaining pits (138 and 163) had both been heavily truncated by later features and produced no artefactual material and no evidence as to their function.

Medieval, Phase 6: Timber slot, ditch and cobble spread (mid 12th century)

Aligned from north to south at the northern end of the trench there was a linear slot (140) (Fig 9). The slot, which was approximately 3.5m long, 0.35m wide and 0.21m deep, had rounded terminals and a shallow

rectangular section (Plate 4). The base of the slot almost certainly held an oak timber, fragments of which were partly preserved. The fills of the slot (120, 160 and 161) contained organic remains consistent with the presence of significant quantities of waste, although there appears to have also been a considerable input of animal dung and foul rotting matter. Several sherds of 11th to 12th-century pottery were recovered from fill 120.

Running from north to south along the eastern edge of the trench was the western edge of a possible ditch or gully (143). At the northern end of the trench the ditch was narrow, being only 0.25m wide and 0.14m deep, but towards the centre and southern end of the trench the ditch (216) became wider and deeper, and the eastern edge of the ditch lay under the trench edge. The fill (133) of the ditch in the northern half of the trench contained a caddis larval case and *Daphnia* ephippia, suggesting that this ditch probably contained water, at least periodically.

At some point the ditch appeared to have been partly recut or cleaned out, or pits were cut into the top of the ditch fill. The interpretation of this later activity is uncertain due to modern disturbance around the concrete pile in the centre of the trench. The pile cut through the centre of a possible pit (145), and a feature immediately to the south of the pile, interpreted as pit 149, may in fact have been part of pit 145. The pottery sherds recovered from the fill (116) of pit 149 included a sherd of Nottingham Splashed ware, which dates from between 1100 and 1230, one of the latest fabric types represented in the pottery assemblage from this site.

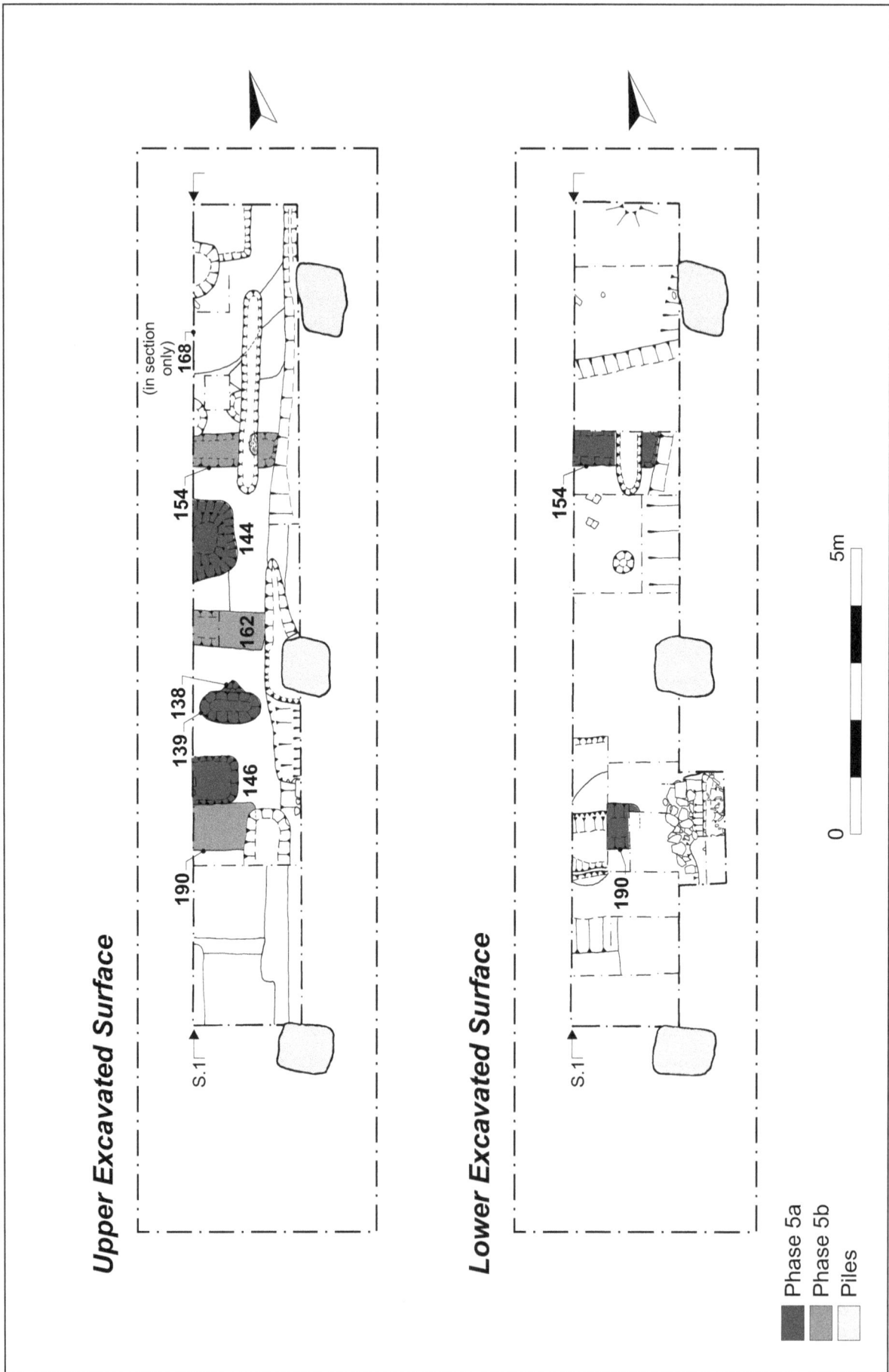

Fig 8: Phase 5, timber building and pits (mid 12th century)

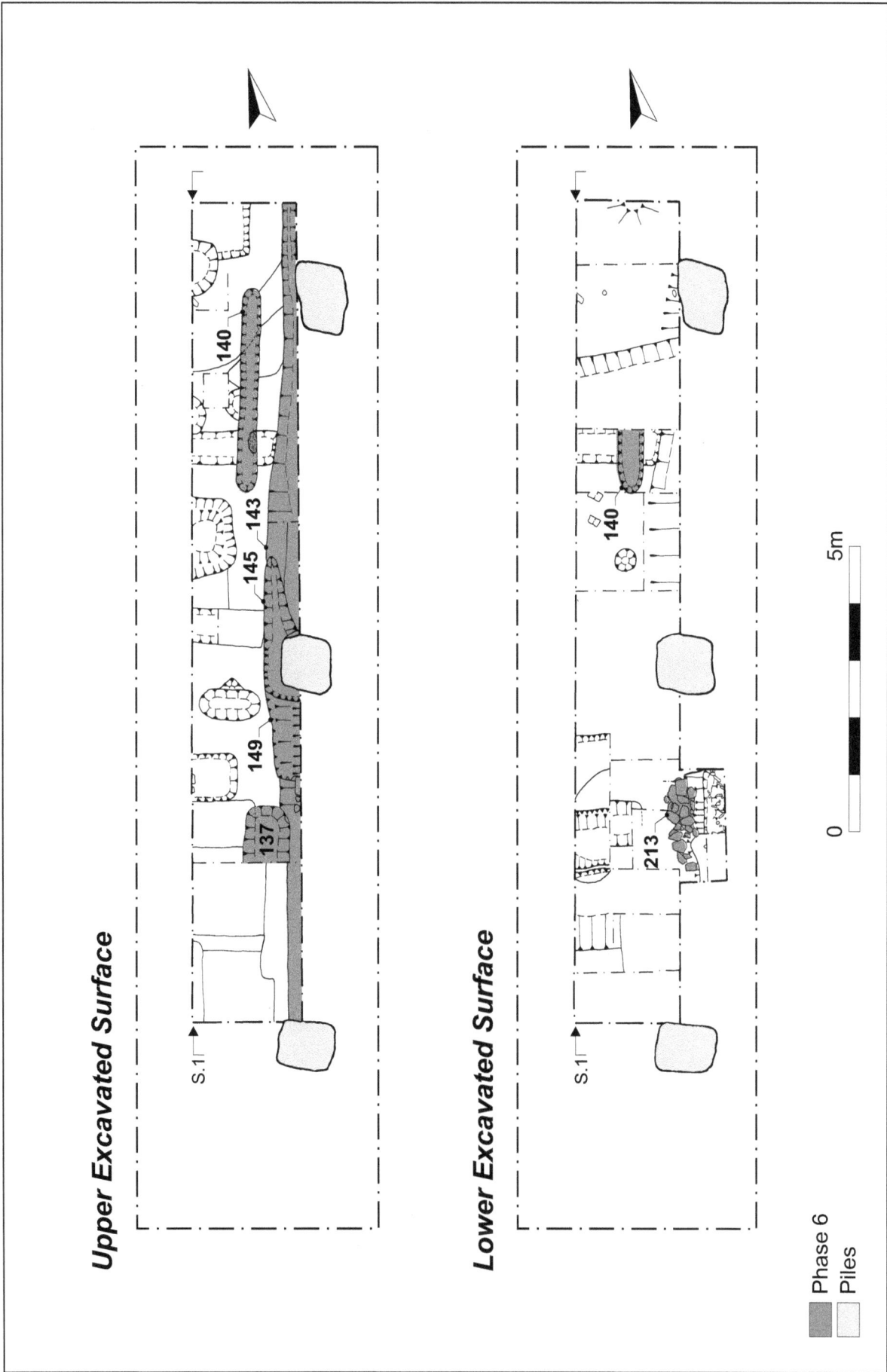

Fig 9: Phase 6, timber slot, ditch and cobble spread (mid 12th century)

Upper Excavated Surface

Lower Excavated Surface

S.1

140

143

145

149

137

213

Phase 6

Piles

5m

0

Upper Excavated Surface

S.1

Lower Excavated Surface

S.1

212
209
210

Wooden stakes **214**

0   5m

Phase 7
Piles

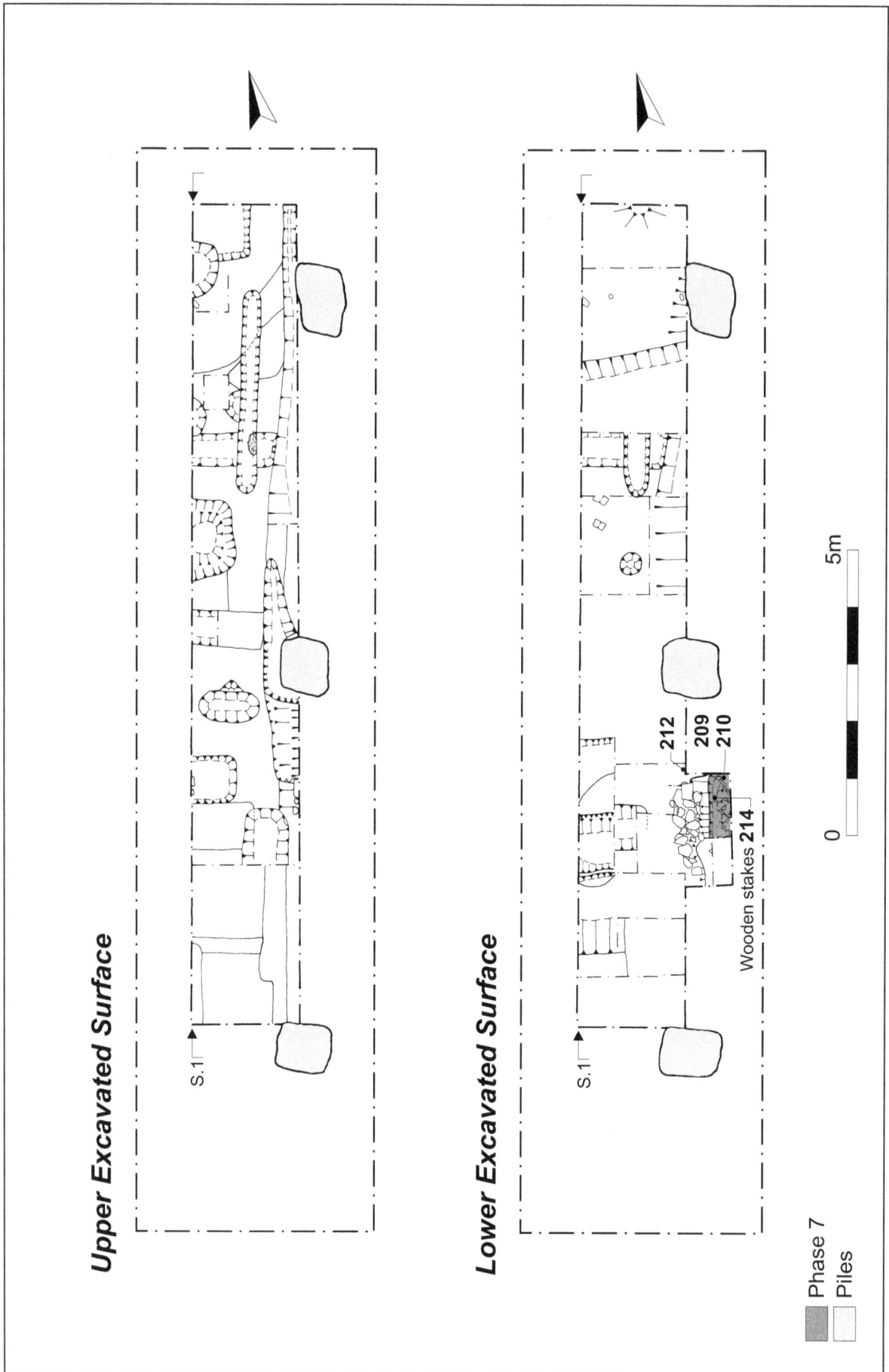

Fig 10: Phase 7, land reclamation (late 12th century)

A pit (137), a shallow, roughly sub-rectangular feature with almost vertical sides and a flat base, was cut into the southern length of ditch 143. The pit, the southern part of which was removed by machine for the excavation of the southern sondage, was at least 1.0m long, 0.85m wide and 0.16m deep. The upper fill (108) contained two sherds of an 11th to 12th-century bowl.

During excavation along the eastern edge of the trench a spread of limestone cobbles (213) was identified, embedded in the top of the fills of ditch 216 and pit 149 (Plate 5). It was decided to excavate a sondage by hand in the eastern edge of the trench to investigate the cobble spread. Excavation revealed that the cobbles (213) formed a roughly sub-rectangular spread extending over an area of approximately 1.7m north to south by 0.5m east to west. The cobbles were angular and sub-angular in shape and up to 300mm in any one dimension. One of

Plate 5: Cobble spread, facing north

the cobbles had been burnt along one edge, indicating possible re-use. The purpose of the cobbles is uncertain. It may have formed an area of consolidated ground at a threshold, or perhaps have formed an area of 'hard-standing' for a structure, such as a trough. It is unlikely to have formed part of any building.

Medieval, phase 7: Land reclamation (late 12th century)

Overlying the cobbles (213) were two layers, 210 and 209 (Fig 10). The earliest of these (210) was c 0.5m thick and contained the remains of wooden stakes and a post, presumably driven into the layer from above, although it is possible that the layer accumulated around them. The stakes were spaced at fairly regular intervals, approximately 0.05m apart, and survived to an average length of c 0.3m (Plate 6). Many of the stakes had worked points at their base and they had diameters ranging from 32-46mm. The stakes could have been part of a wattle hurdle, perhaps secured in place by the post, which had a diameter of 75mm; however, there was no evidence for the wattles.

Plate 6: Wooden stakes (213) in west-facing section

The deposit also contained lenses, up to 300mm long and 60mm thick, of degraded mortar, which formed a tip line in the central region of the layer. Layer 210 also contained a thin band of charcoal-rich ashy silt (211).

Soil samples from the layers contained abundant charcoal and charred cereal, probably from domestic fires. Pottery sherds typically dated to the late 11th to late 12th centuries, and included a sherd from a large vessel with a flat-topped rim, possibly a large jar (Fig 11), a type previously unknown in Lincoln.

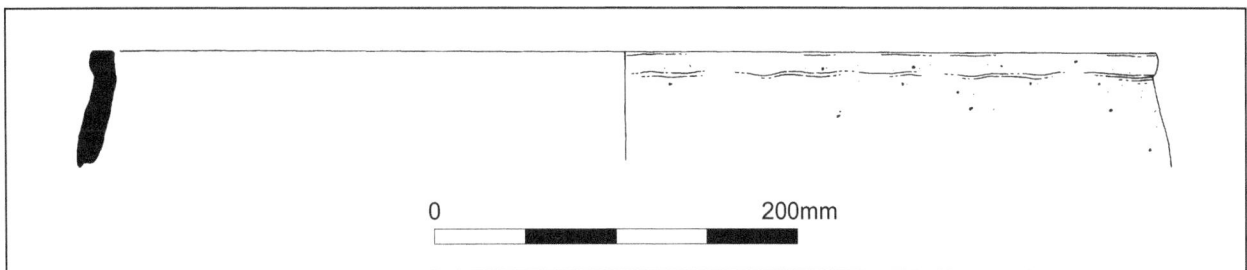

0   200mm

Fig 11: A large medieval jar, layer 210

Upper Excavated Surface

Lower Excavated Surface

Phase 8
Piles

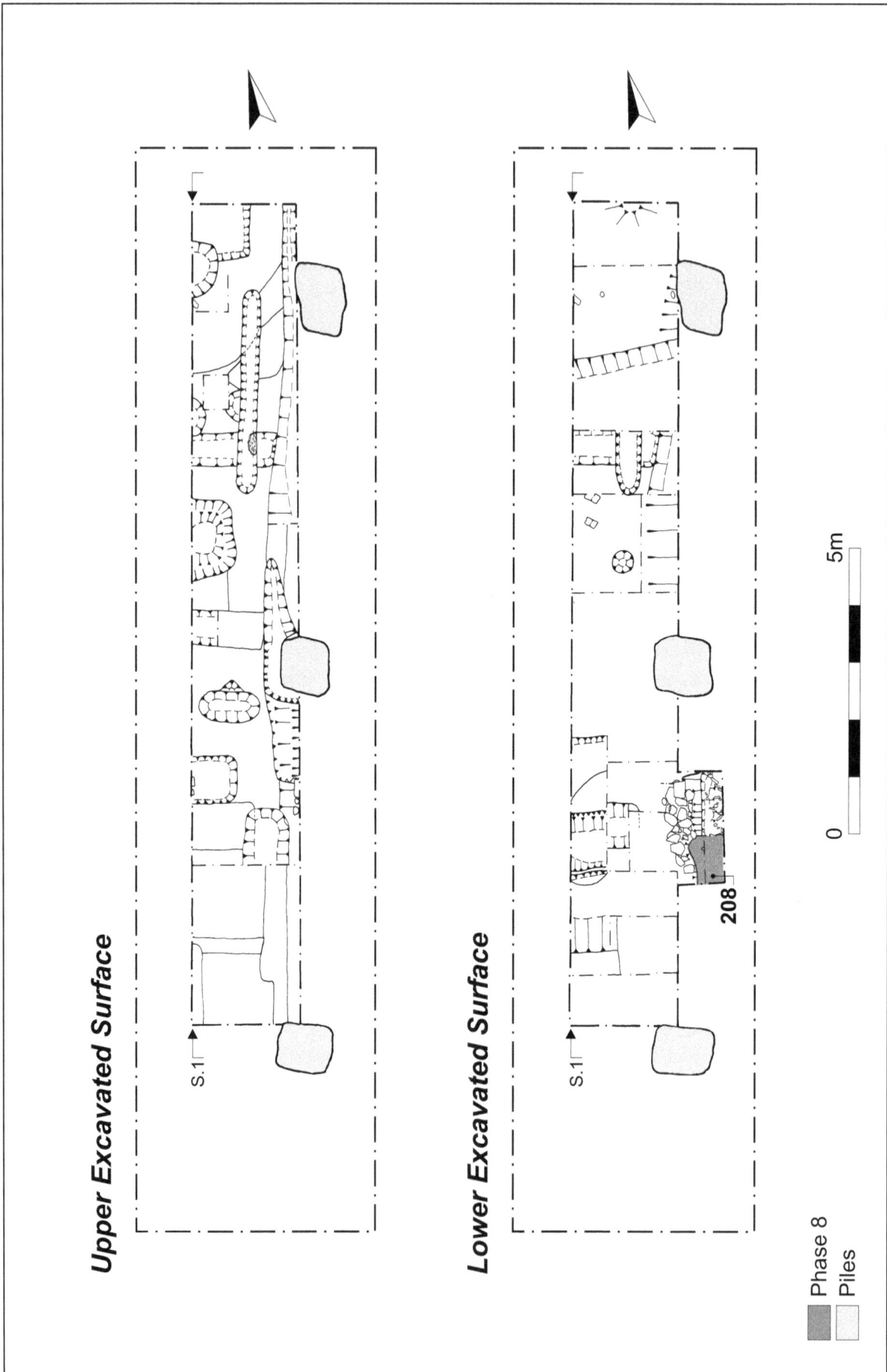

Fig 12: Phase 8, later medieval soil horizon

Layer 209 was cut by a large pit (212), most of which had been removed during the excavation of the trench. The northern end of the pit had been destroyed by the central concrete pile. The surviving portion of the pit was 0.62m deep with primary and secondary fills (207 and 206). No dating evidence was forthcoming, although small lenses of mortar were evident in the upper fill (206). The purpose of the pit is unknown.

Medieval, phase 8: Dark soil horizon (later medieval)

The latest deposit on the site beneath the modern demolition layers was a layer, approximately 0.3m thick, of dark brown, almost black silt (208) (Fig 12). The layer only survived in the central eastern section of the trench, where truncation of archaeological levels by modern development was less severe. The layer is undated, but overlay pit 212, which probably dates to the 12th century, suggesting that the layer is of a similar or later medieval date. No comparable deposits are detailed in the report of the excavations in the 1970s.

Modern deposits

The medieval remains were sealed by modern layers 101 and 100, modern development on the site presumably having truncated any later medieval or post-medieval remains (Fig 3).

The modern layers, comprising brick and concrete demolition rubble, were 1.6m thick at the southern end of the trench and 1.2m thick at the northern end. The building material typically derived from the 19th and 20th-century buildings that formerly occupied the site. In addition to these layers there were three large concrete piles surviving from the latest structure, which was built in the 1970s. The piles cut through the archaeological horizons and penetrated to an unknown depth.

Chapter 3: The finds

The Roman pottery
by Margaret J Darling

Only four residual sherds of Roman pottery, deriving from four contexts, were recovered from the site. The pottery has been archived according to the guidelines of *The Study Group for Roman Pottery*. The pottery consists of:

Layer 106	Central Gaulish samian form 31, footring, 1 sherd
Layer 113	Central Gaulish samian body sherd from a decorated form, probably a form 37, the decoration being non-identifiable, 1 sherd
Slot 140 fill 120	Grey, fairly sandy fabric, shoulder sherd from a jar or bowl, not closely datable but probably 1st to 3rd century rather than 4th century, 1 sherd
Pit 144 fill 131	Central Gaulish samian, rim fragment of a probable form 31, 1 sherd

Given that the grey body sherd cannot be closely dated, the other three sherds would fit into the later 2nd century.

The medieval pottery
by Jane Young

A total of 107 sherds of medieval pottery were recovered from the site. The material ranges in date from the late 10th to the 12th centuries. The pottery was examined visually and then recorded using locally and nationally agreed codenames. The assemblage was quantified by three measures: number of sherds, weight and vessel count within each context. The pottery data was entered on an Access database.

The material is in variable condition with most vessels being slightly abraded. Little of the pottery is discoloured or shows evidence of having been deposited in waterlaid deposits. A number of sherds have thick internal and external soot deposits that suggest they were acquired post-breakage. None of the material is typical of primary deposition.

A suggested date range for the deposition of each strat-ified context is shown in Table 1; however, the almost complete absence of the main early to mid/late

Table 1: Suggested deposition date of stratified pottery groups from contexts

Phase	Feature	Context	No. of sherds	No. of vessels	Weight (g)	Date (centuries AD)
1	Layer	113	8	6	36	mid/late 11th to mid 12th
1	Layer	172	4	4	8	mid to late 11th
2	Pit 158	125	2	2	17	mid 11th to mid 12th
2	Ditch 186	185	9	9	26	early/mid 11th to mid/late 12th
2	Ditch 188	187	1	1	10	early/mid 11th to mid/late 12th
3	Pit 157	129	4	3	8	late 11th to mid/late 12th
3	Ditch 191	112	2	2	6	late 10th to mid/late 12th
3	Ditch 191	128	6	6	52	mid 11th to mid/late 12th
3	Ditch 193	194	2	1	11	mid 11th to mid/late 12th
4	Layer	106	9	9	53	late 11th to mid 12th
5a	Ditch 154	121	1	1	3	early/mid 11th to mid 12th
5b	Pit 139	105	7	7	17	mid/late 11th to mid/late 12th
5b	Pit 144	131	9	8	155	late 11th to early/mid 12th
5b	Pit 144	141	2	2	10	mid 11th to mid/late 12th
5b	Ditch 146	127	9	8	62	late 11th to mid 12th
5b	Ditch 146	107	5	5	64	late 11th to mid 12th
6	Ditch 137	108	2	1	86	early to mid 12th
6	Slot 140	120	5	4	74	late 11th to mid 12th
6	Ditch 143	133	1	1	3	late 10th to mid/late 12th
6	Pit 145	103	8	6	39	early to mid/late 12th
6	Pit 149	116	3	3	20	early to mid 12th
7	Layer	210	5	5	103	late 10th to mid/late 12th
7	Layer	211	1	1	1	mid 11th to mid/late 12th

Table 2: Pottery codenames and total quantities by sherd, weight (g) and vessel count

Codename	Full name	No. of sherds	Weight (g)	No. of vessels	earliest date AD	latest date AD
EMHM	Early Medieval Handmade ware	1	7	1	1100	1230
LFS	Lincolnshire Fine-shelled ware	68	522	61	970	1200
LFS/ELFS	Lincolnshire Fine-shelled or Early Fine-shelled	1	83	1	780	1200
NSP	Nottingham Splashed ware	1	10	1	1100	1230
SNLS	Saxo-Norman Lincoln Sandy Ware	1	6	1	970	1080
SNX	Non-local Saxo-Norman Fabrics	1	44	1	870	1150
ST	Stamford Ware	26	147	24	970	1200
STCRUC	Stamford-type Crucible	1	4	1	850	1150
THETT	Thetford-type fabrics	1	29	1	1000	1150
YG	Yorkshire gritty ware	2	8	1	1050	1250

11th-century pottery types found in the city (Torksey ware and Lincoln Saxo-Norman Sandy ware) from the overall assemblage indicates that deposition did not take place until at least the last quarter of the 11th century. The small amount of identifiable 12th-century material suggests that the assemblage does not date later than the mid 12th century. The entire assemblage could belong to a short period between the late 11th and early/mid 12th centuries, with the latest material coming from fill 116 of pit 149.

Ten different medieval pottery ware types were found on the site; the type and date range for each fabric are shown in Table 2. The majority of the pottery is of Lincolnshire Fine-Shelled ware, the main coarseware in use in Lincoln between the mid 11th and mid 12th centuries. One of the sherds of this fabric comes from a large, flat-rimmed vessel (Fig 11), a form previously unknown in Lincoln. The second most common pottery type is Stamford ware, used for both domestic and tableware. No evidence for the finer early/mid 12th-century and later Stamford fabrics was found on the site. One Stamford ware vessel is a small biconical crucible, typical of those found on sites in the city in deposits dating to the last quarter of the 11th century. Apart from the crucible, identifiable vessel form types in all fabrics are limited to jars, bowls and jug/pitchers.

The material recovered represents a small mixed assemb-

lage, mainly of late 11th to mid 12th-century date. It is probable that this material was deposited as part of reclamation attempts in the area during this period.

The ceramic building material
by Jane Young

A total of 19 fragments (510g) of ceramic building material were recovered from the site (Table 3). The pottery and tile was examined visually and then recorded using locally and nationally agreed codenames. All of the material broadly dates to the Roman period, with the exception of one fragment from fill 116 of pit 149, which has a wide date range from 1100 to 1900.

The non-ceramic finds
by Tora Hylton

A few 'small finds' were recovered from deposits dating to the late 10th to mid/late 12th centuries. Objects worthy of note include a whetstone and a spindle whorl, both manufactured from fine-grained siltstone. The whetstone, from buried soil horizon 106, was incomplete, however, the presence of a perforation indicates that originally it would have been suspended from the waist and used as a personal hone for sharpening knives. The spindle whorl came from pit 146 (fill 127), the pit possibly lying inside a timber building, and would have been used for hand-spinning yarn. The other objects include two residual

Table 3: Summary of tile by context

Phase	Feature	Context	Code	Full name	No. of frags	Weight (g)
1	Layer	166	RBRK	Roman brick	1	80
1	Layer	172	RTIL	Roman tile	4	7
1	Layer	172	TEG	Tegula	1	173
2	Pit 158	125	RTIL	Roman tile	1	6
2	Ditch 188	187	RTIL	Roman tile	4	8
3	Pit 152	153	RBRK	Roman brick	1	9
5b	Ditch 146	127	RTIL	Roman tile	1	2
6	Ditch 137	108	TEG	Tegula	1	33
6	Pit 149	116	PNR	Peg, nib or ridge tile	1	82
6	Slot 140	120	RBRK	Roman brick	1	85

probable early Neolithic flint flakes (Alex Thorne pers comm), two iron nails, and an undiagnostic strip of iron.

Nail. Iron, complete. T-shaped head with squared section shank and clenched terminal. Length 35mm. Mid to late 11th century. Layer 172, phase 1, soil sample 17

Strip of iron, possibly a billet, with parallel sides and rectangular cross-section. Heavily encrusted in corrosion products. Length 40mm, width 8mm, thickness 4mm. Early/mid 11th to mid/late 12th centuries. Ditch 188, context 187, phase 2, soil sample 14

Whetstone, fine-grained siltstone, incomplete, one terminal missing. Sub-triangular cross-section with three smooth sides. Partially drilled perforation on one side and five tiny knifepoint-sharpening grooves on the others. Late 11th to mid 12th centuries. Length 47mm, width 16mm, thickness 10mm. Layer 106, phase 4

Spindle whorl, fine-grained siltstone, complete. Biconical discoid whorl with large central perforation. The perforation is slightly waisted; it has been drilled from both sides. Diameter 37mm, thickness 10mm, diameter of perforation 10mm. Late 11th to mid 12th centuries. Pit 146 context 127, phase 5, soil sample 10

Nail, incomplete. Flat-headed nail with square-sectioned shank, terminal missing. Measurements: head 15 x 40mm, shank (incomplete) 17mm. Late 10th to mid/late 12th centuries. Ditch 143, context 133, phase 6, soil sample 18

The leather
by June Swann

A small amount of leather was collected from three contexts, which seem to represent, at the most, fragments of four items of footwear. The items were not retained.

Part of repair patch, 58 x 37mm. One side is the original semicircular edge, with five pairs and part of a sixth pair of tunnel stitch-holes, close to the edge. The opposite

edge is broken, making it impossible to say whether it was a small patch or a half sole clump as that from context 102. The pair of holes are at 14mm distance, and the shortness of the tunnel suggests a sole, and quite fine work. Its rounded shape is more likely to be for a sole heel-seat than for a medieval toe end, though some 11th-century soles are almost as round as this. Its comparative thinness does not rule out its use as a patch for the upper. Late 11th to mid 12th centuries. Pit 157, context 129, phase 3

Tiny fragment of leather, 12 x 8mm. Late 11th to mid/late 12th centuries. Pit 157, context 129, phase 3, soil sample 6, small find SF6

Left clump sole, about 133 x 76mm. Probably oval toe, now damaged. Broken across waist, though scallop effect suggests it was attached to a flexible sole (as expected for medieval shoes) and pulled away from the stitches during wear. Tunnel stitch-holes (as used to attach clump sole repairs) at toe, outside edge and possibly waist; broken away on inside edge. Pair of holes for the thread at approximately 17mm, set close to the edge (closer than normal, as more commonly found for repairs in the later Middle Ages to the 16th century). Repair sole worn right through across tread for 50mm from right (broken) edge; 12mm wide at widest, and closer to outside joint (the greatest wear is usually under the inside, big toe joint). This suggests a foot problem, probably 'treading over' on the outside joint. Mid 12th century. Pit 144, context 102, phase 5

Part of leather upper, 50 x 42mm. 16mm original edge with two holes straight through the leather, for attaching to sole, about 7mm stitch length. With differential shrinkage, it might belong with the sole fragment above. Mid 12th century. Pit 144, context 102, phase 5

Fragment of sole, 50 x 41mm. One original straight edge 25mm long, with four edge-flesh stitch-holes, 6mm stitch length; part of lasting margin delaminated and broken away. Mid 12th century. Timber slot 140, context 120, phase 6

Chapter 4: Environmental Evidence

by James Rackham

(with John Giorgi, David Smith, Michelle Morris, Rowena Gale, John Carrott, Alison Locker and Karen Deighton)

Introduction

Excavations on the development site on the north bank of Brayford Pool, Lincoln were conducted in three phases, comprising an initial test-pit evaluation, a small single trench excavation and a subsequent watching brief. Animal bone was recovered from all three phases of work and environmental samples were taken from the evaluation and the excavation phases. Soil sample assessment reports and animal bone assessments were produced for all stages of work (Rackham 2001; Deighton 2001a, 2001b). This report specifically details the results from the post-excavation analysis of the environmental material collected during the main excavation phase conducted by Northamptonshire Archaeology.

The excavated trench lay within the area of ground reclaimed from Brayford Pool in the Saxo-Norman period and the excavations uncovered elements of the first occupation of the site. The stratigraphic seqence has been assigned to eight phases of activity and the material reported on below is all derived from deposits dated to the late 11th to late 12th centuries AD. Many of these deposits were waterlogged and the environmental assessment has noted the exceptional preservation in some deposits (Rackham 2001).

The assessment indicated two key areas of investigation that could be targeted during the post-excavation analysis:

1   the interpretation of the origin and composition of some of the deposits, particularly those that might represent buried ground surfaces or ground made up to raise the ground level above the water in the Pool
2   the function of specific features and the range of food items consumed at the site.

A total of 19 soil samples and 404 hand-collected bone fragments were recovered from the excavation. The samples were taken from a range of feature types with the best sampled features being pit fills (seven samples), followed by ditch/gully fills (six samples), levelling layers (two samples) and one sample from a slot. The size of the samples ranged from 11 to 30 litres, although the majority were over 20 litres. The manner in which the soil samples were processed is detailed in the assessment report (Rackham 2001). A summary of the archaeological finds from the samples and the size of individual samples are shown in Tables 4 and 5 (pp. 24-26).

Core samples

As part of the programme of investigation the Environmental Archaeology Consultancy also extracted two cores through the deposits below the excavated horizons to establish the character and sequence of the sediments infilling Brayford Pool at this location.

The two cores were sunk at the northern and southern ends of the excavation trench. The cores were taken using a 1 metre, 2.5cm diameter gouge auger. Borehole 1 (BH1) was commenced at a level of approximately 3.5m OD; unfortunately, a precise level for the top of this core was not recorded. Borehole 2 (BH2) started at a level of 3.20m OD. The sediments observed in BH1 were recorded and briefly described in the field. Those from BH2 were taken as a continuous sequence of 100mm samples from the top to the base of the sequence and two radiocarbon samples were submitted from this latter sequence. The radiocarbon dates obtained from the samples are given below.

The natural sedimentary sequence

The lowest deposits in both cores are fine to medium grey sands with occasional organic fragments and pieces of wood (probably rootwood). Previous work around Brayford Pool has indicated that these sands represent the natural deposits of the area. In BH2 the sands are overlain by a thin (0.13m) layer of laminated organic silts. These first occur at 0.65m OD and may be lacustrine in origin. Above these deposits a thick woody peat bed developed, probably indicative of a fen carr type habitat. Peats of this type occur in both cores at a similar level. A sample from BH2 at 0.85-0.95m OD, at the base of the peats in this core, was submitted for radiocarbon analysis and has produced a date of 3020±60 BP (see above), indicating a late Bronze Age date for the onset of peat development in this area. At approximately 1.4m OD the peats become fibrous, continuing in BH2 for a further 0.8m. In BH1 these peats are interdigitated with deposits of organic sands. The location of this borehole on the uphill side

Source	Depth (m)	OD height (m)	Laboratory number	Measured age BP	Calibrated date (95% confidence)
BH2	0.86-0.96	2.22-2.32	Beta-157533	1260±60	Cal AD 660-900
BH2	2.23-2.33	0.85-0.95	Beta-157534	3020±60	Cal BC 1410-1060

Table 4: Finds from the environmental samples

Sample no.	Phase	Feature	Context	Sample volume (l)	Organic residue volume (ml)	Pot sherds/weight (g)	Pebble gravel weight (g)	Brick/tile weight (g)	Lime-stone weight (g)	Metal	Marine shell weight (g)	Bone weight (g)	Other ¢
19	7	layer	210	10	400	3/8	21	+	157	-	18	43	slag
8	7	layer 210	211	10	1200	1/1	95	1	57	-	13	47	hammerscale and a little slag
18	6	ditch 143	133	20	800	1/3	59	+	100	1xFe	36	22	nail, fired stone, hammerscale
3	6	slot 140	160	11	4000	-	-	-	-	-	3	74	2 pieces fine leather in flot, wooden object
1	5B	pit 139	105	24	>3000	6/9	57	-	169	-	18	31	2 flint flakes
9	5B	pit 144	131	24	7000	-	-	+	62	-	20	175	
15	5B	pit 146	107	3.5	300	2/7	4	-	68	-	1	2	
10	5B	pit 146	127	20	3500	6/19	6	1	90	-	18	148	possible hammerstone?, spindle whorl
2	5A	slot 190	156	13	3000	-	9	-	20	-	9	19	
4	4	layer	106	22	800	3/6	9	+	171	-	22	39	
7	3	pit 152	153	18	1000	-	16	+	200	-	8	23	coal
6	3	pit 157	129	24	4000	3/7	18	-	147	-	85	75	1 piece leather
5	2	pit 158	125	23	2000	1/8	63	+	38	-	2	129	
16	2	pit 203	170	18	700	-	355	-	-	-	+	-	
13	2	ditch 186	185	22	1000	6/15	12	+	53	-	15	7	
11	3	ditch 191	112	30	3500	1/1	23	-	330	-	52	187	
12	3	ditch 191	128	27	3000	4/16	56	+	175	-	82	200	1 piece leather
14	2	ditch 188	187	21	3000	1/8	56	9	173	1xFe	99	74	
17	1	layer	172	12	1200	4/7	114	11	62	1xFe	88	56	nail

+ present in quantities below 1g

All finds sorted from >7mm fractions unless otherwise indicated

¢ some sorted from >2mm fraction

suggests that these sands are being washed downslope, forming lake edge and wash deposits around the margins of the Pool, but not extending as far as BH2. These wash deposits probably reflect activity and ground disturbance upslope from this point and may have formed in the Roman period or even earlier.

At the top of the peats in BH2 a sample taken from the organic sands immediately overlying the peats has given a date Cal AD 660-900, indicating that peat formation at this location had ceased by the Saxon period. The overlying sands with fibrous and humified organic matter within them appear likely to represent a combination of *in situ* organic sediment formation and inwashed sands from the adjacent terrestrial deposits. This influx of sands continued above, although less rapidly, with sandy silts and degraded organic sediments forming beneath the first archaeological horizons which have been dated to the mid-

Table 5a: Environmental finds from the samples

Sample no.	Feature	Context no.	Sample volume (l)	Flot volume (ml)	Charcoal *	Wood *	Water-logged seed*	Insect *	Puparia	Water flea *	Rootlet	Fish *	Egg-shell *	Snail *	Interp. $
19	210	210	10	30	4	+	4	-	-	2	-	1	2	1	
8	210	211	10	300	5	-	5	2	-	3	-	2	1	1	
18	143	133	20	180	4	4	4	2	++	3	+	-	2	-	
3	140	160	11	500	-	5	5	5	++++	-	-	-	1	-	cess
1	139	105	24	1000	1	4	5	4	++	2	-	1	-	-	
9	144	131	24	800	1	4	5	5	++++	2	-	1	-	-	cess
15	146	107	3.5	80	3	3	3	3	++	-	-	2	-	-	
10	146	127	20	500	2	5	5	4	++	-	+	1	-	-	
2	190	156	13	400	2	5	5	4	++	3	+	-	-	-	
4	Lev	106	22	100	2	3	4	2		4	++++	2	-	1	veget.
7	152	153	18	85	1	3	4	2	++	5	++	-	-	1	
6	157	129	24	400	5	4	5	4	++	2		1	-	2	
5	158	125	23	250	3	-	4	3		2	++	-	-	4	
16	203	170	18	150	2	2	3	2		2	+++++	-	-	1	veget .
13	186	185	22	300	4	2	4	3		5	++++	1	1	-	veget.
11	191	112	30	1100	2	5	5	5	++++	2		1	-	-	cess
12	191	128	27	800	4	3	5	5	++++	4	++	-	1	-	cess
14	188	187	21	900	2	4	4	4	++	-	++	-	-	-	
17	Lev	172	12	180	2	2	4	?		2	++++			2	veget. fore-shore?

frequency; 1= 1-10; 2 = 11-50; 3 = 51-150; 4=151-250; 5 =>250 items
+ present grading to +++++ very abundant.
$ probable contemporary vegetated ground surface

late 11th century. The degraded and humified character of these upper organic deposits implies that the sediments dried out for a time in the Late Saxon period, and this may have lead to the expansion of settlement across the area and the formation of the archaeological horizons. Changes in the watertable appear to have continued, with the lowest archaeological horizons becoming sufficiently waterlogged to preserve organic remains in exceptional condition. Thin but well defined lenses of sand in the upper levels of BH1 appear to reflect episodes of slopewash at the northern end of the excavation trench. It is probable that the sands in the upper half of both sequences could be equated with ground disturbance in the Middle and Late Saxon period.

Plant remains
by John Giorgi

Introduction

The waterlogged and charred flots of 16 of the 19 samples were submitted for the analysis of the plant remains. Identifications were carried out using a binocular microscope together with modern and charred reference material and reference manuals. All the samples had been stored wet owing to the good organic preservation of the remains. The individual flots were wet-sieved through a stack of sieves and scanned wet although the quantity of remains in the samples meant that many of the smaller fractions (1mm, 0.5mm, 0.25mm sieves) were subdivided because there was insufficient time to scan the whole flot; between 25% and 50% of fractions below 1mm were examined in 11 samples while fractions of 25% were examined in four samples below 0.5mm.

The presence and frequency of plant items preserved by waterlogging was recorded without being sorted (with the exception of remains that were not readily identifiable). Cereal grains and weed seeds were sorted and quantified while estimates of the frequency of the waterlogged species, charcoal fragments, charred stems and small grass seeds were made on the basis of the following code: + = 1-10; ++ = 11-50; +++ = 51-150; ++++ = > 150 items.

Results

Organic preservation of plant remains was exceptionally good, with all the samples producing large quantities of botanical material preserved mainly by waterlogging. A smaller assemblage of charred plant remains was recovered, consisting largely of wood charcoal (flecks, small fragments, twigs) in all samples, plus a relatively smaller quantity of cereal grains, weed seeds and a few stem fragments. The results are shown in Tables 6-8.

Table 5b: Environmental finds from the samples

Sample	Feature	Context	Sample Volume (l)	Flot volume (ml)	Interp. $	preliminary identification of some of the finds
19	210	210	10	30		sheep, pig, goose, mussel, cockle, degraded wood, charred grain (oat?, wheat?), elder (very abundant), goosefoots, *Planorbis vortex*, etc
8	210	211	10	300		cattle, sheep, bird, eel, herring, mussel, oyster, cockle, charred grain – oat, barley?, wheat?, elder (very abundant), blackberry/raspberry, charred seeds, *Bithynia tentaculata*, etc
18	143	133	20	180		sheep, cattle, chicken, mussel, cockle, periwinkle, degraded wood, elder, goosefoots, caddis larvae, etc
3	140	160	11	500	cess	horn core, mussels, small roundwood, split/worked wood, many twigs, plum, cherry, bullace?, grain, moss, flower, straw/hay, etc
1	139	105	24	1000		pig, sheep, cattle, mussel, small roundwood, twigs, worked/split wood, hair, elder, goosefoots, moss, hay/straw?, etc
9	144	131	24	800	cess	cattle, pig, sheep, chicken, mussel, cockle, fruit stones, elder, moss, straw/hay, small roundwood, many twigs, etc
15	146	107	3.5	80		mussel, small roundwood, twigs, thorns (sloe/hawthorn?), hazelnut, fruitstone, elder, heather?, goosefoots, moss, charred grain, charred heather?, charred flower buds, etc
10	146	127	20	500		cattle, pig, sheep, chicken, mussel, oyster, small roundwood, wood, bark, many twigs, moss, heather?, buds, elder, etc
2	190	156	13	400		sheep, mussels, chaff, wood, small roundwood, shavings, split roundwood, many small twigs, elder, moss, dog turd, etc
4	Lev	106	22	100	veget.	sheep, pig, mussel, cockle, oyster, wood, twigs, chopped wood, *Succinea* sp., *Planorbis* sp., charred oat, elder, goosefoots, coprolite, etc
7	152	153	18	85		cattle, goose, mussel, cockle, small roundwood, twigs, elder, hazelnuts, *Planorbis vortex*, etc
6	157	129	24	400		pig, sheep, mussel, oyster, cockle, goose, small roundwood, chopped wood, shavings, small roundwood, many twigs, hazelnuts, buds, hay/straw, *Planorbis* sp. *Sphaerium* sp., *Succinea* sp., etc
5	158	125	23	250		cattle, mussel, oyster, cockle, charred grain, elder, goosefoot, blackberry/raspberry, caddis, leach eggs, *Planorbis vortex*, *P. corneus*, *P. contortus*, *P. albus*, *Lymnaea* sp, *Valvata cristata*, *Bithynia tentaculata*, *Pisidium* sp., etc
16	203	170	18	150	veget .	small roundwood, *Bithynia* sp., etc
13	186	185	22	300	veget.	cattle, pig, mussel, periwinkle, cockle, small twigs, elder, goosefoots, moss, etc
11	191	112	30	1100	cess	cattle, sheep, pig, mussel, oyster, cockle, small roundwood, twigs, thorns (sloe/hawthorn?), plum, bullace?, cherry, hazelnut, goosefoots, moss, possible bran, etc
12	191	128	27	800	cess	cattle, pig, sheep, mussel, oyster, cockle, periwinkle, small roundwood, shavings?, twigs, thorns (sloe/hawthorn?), plum, hazelnuts, cherry, goosefoots, moss, flower, possible bran, etc
14	188	187	21	900		cattle, sheep, pig, bird, mussel, whelk, cockle, periwinkle, oyster, small roundwood, shavings?, twigs, dog turd?, hazelnut, plum, moss, flower buds?, etc
17	Lev	172	12	180	veget . fore-shore?	cattle, sheep, pig, mussel, oyster, cockle, periwinkle, grain?, degraded wood, hazelnut, elder, moss, leach egg?, *Bithynia tentaculata*, *Lymnaea peregra*, *Viviparous fasciatus*, etc

frequency; 1= 1-10; 2 = 11-50; 3 = 51-150; 4=151-250; 5 =>250 items
+ present grading to +++++ very abundant.
$ probable contemporary vegetated ground surface

The waterlogged plant remains consisted of large numbers of fruits and seeds, representing mainly wild plants but including a number of potential economic (mainly food) species. Other botanical material included large amounts of fragmented wood in all samples, much of which consisted of small roundwood and twigs but also shavings and bark. Stem fragments of different sizes were present in most samples; some of the round, hollow, ribbed stems may belong to grasses including cereals. Other stems were smaller and not so diagnostic and may belong to a range of plants represented in the samples. Mosses were well represented in virtually every sample while moderate quantities of buds were noted in six samples with a few thorns in others, some of which may belong to the wild fruits represented in the samples (see below). Rootlets were also present in a number of samples, occasionally in large quantities.

Detailed examination, however, was restricted mainly to the fruits and seeds because the author had neither the time nor resources to identify the other remains, although comments will be made on this material if it has a bearing on the interpretation of the other plant remains in an assemblage.

Economic plants

Economic plants were represented mainly by charred cereal grains, cereal bran, fruit stones, fruit seeds and seeds of cultivated flax (*Linum usitatissimum*). The majority of these remains probably represent food residues.

CEREALS

Cereals were represented on the site by a small assemblage of about 150 charred grains, which were found in virtually every sample (the richest samples being 50 grains in pit fill 125 and 21 grains in ditch fill 112), plus large quantities of cereal bran in five samples. The grains included wheat (*Triticum* spp.), barley (*Hordeum sativum*) and oats (*Avena* spp.) in most samples, and two rye (*Secale cereale*) grains in two samples. However, almost half of the grains were too poorly preserved to be identified.

Oats were the best-represented cereal with the identification of two florets showing the presence of cultivated oat (*Avena sativa*) in the samples. The well-preserved barley grains showed the presence of six-row hulled grain, while the well-preserved wheat grains, with a rounded squat morphology, suggests the presence of free-threshing bread/club wheat (*Triticum aestivum*). The cereal bran was extremely fragmentary, generally smaller than 0.5mm. Some of the waterlogged and charred stem fragments in the samples may also belong to cereals although it is difficult to differentiate between the stems of large grasses and cereals (van der Veen 1991).

The cereals represented in the samples, free-threshing wheat, barley, oats and rye, are the four main grains recovered from medieval sites in England, albeit in variable quantities (Greig 1991, 321). It is not possible, however, to comment on the relative importance of the different cereals at Brayford Pool on the small number of grains in these samples.

All the cereals may have been used on their own (with the exception of oats) or as mixes for bread in the medieval period. Wheaten bread was used for white bread, while rye produced a dark and heavy bread, not so popular with the better off (Wilson 1991, 220). Cereals were also used in pottage, a type of stew, which could also include root vegetables and meat and was the national dish of all classes until the 17th century. Barley (and sometimes oats) was also used for malting, although none of the grains in the samples showed signs of sprouting, good evidence for such a use. Oats and barley were also used as animal fodder.

FLAX

Cultivated flax seeds were found in seven samples, in very large numbers in five of them. Flax had a number of economic uses both as food and as an industrial/ commercial plant.

The fibres of the plant were used in the textile industry for the production of canvas, cloth, and rope (Grieve 1992). Flax stems and capsules were found in early medieval ditch fills from 4-12 Norton Folgate, London (Davis 1997, 18) and in Anglo-Scandinavian deposits from 16-22 Coppergate, York (Kenward and Hall 1995, 773), with the seeds only being secondary evidence for the use of the plant in fibre production.

Stem fragments were indeed found in large numbers in seven samples from Brayford Pool, including thin stems that may be from flax in slot fill 160, pit fill 131 and ditch fill 187, all of which also contained fairly large quantities of flax seeds. However, the stem fragments were not particularly diagnostic and were not examined in detail, so they could belong to other plants in the samples. Moreover, no flax capsules, which are fairly diagnostic, were noted during the scanning of the samples, an absence that cannot be attributed to differential preservation given the good survival of organic material from the site.

Thus, at this site it would be appear that the flax seeds from the Brayford Pool samples are more likely to be food residues. This is also supported by the fact that all five large assemblages of flax seeds were in the same samples as large quantities of bran; flax seeds were sometimes mixed with grain and used in bread before consumption as well as in stews (Greig 1988, 122). Linseed oil from flax seeds was also used in cooking and lighting, and was also used for a range of medicinal purposes, for example as a remedy for coughs and urinary infections (Grieve 1992).

FRUIT

A wide range of fruits was represented in the samples with *Prunus* stones of plum/bullace (*Prunus domestica*), sloe/blackthorn (*P. spinosa*), cherry (*P. avium*), plus hazel (*Corylus avellana*) nut shell, and seeds of apple/crab apple (*Malus domestica/sylvestris*), apple/pear (*Malus/ Pyrus* spp.), blackberry/ raspberry (*Rubus fruticosus/ idaeus*) and elder (*Sambucus nigra*). Large quantities of apple endocarp fragments were also recovered from four samples.

All these species may be from wild plants and may be indicative of the local shrub/hedgerow vegetation rather than the residues of gathered and consumed fruit. Indeed, whole unopened hazel nuts were found in pit fill 131. On the other hand, these fruits would have provided a useful food resource and the quantity of some of the remains suggests so; for example, apple was particularly well represented by endocarp fragments and was a widely cultivated and consumed fruit in the medieval period (Greig 1988), while the plum stones varied quite considerably in size, particularly from slot fill 160, suggesting the presence of a number of possibly cultivated varieties.

Fresh fruit was not eaten widely except by the rich who consumed it (including plums and cherries) as an appetizer to open the stomach at the beginning of a meal. The poor may have relied more on gathering wild fruits. The more common way of consuming fruit was to firstly cook it, fruit being widely used in pottage; for example, apples were boiled and sieved and used in a pottage known as 'appulmos' (Wilson 1991, 334).

OTHER POTENTIAL FOOD PLANTS

A number of plants represented in the samples may have been exploited for food. Low numbers of seeds of *Brassica/Sinapis* species, which includes cabbage, rape, etc., were found in seven samples; these may represent either cultivated or wild vegetables exploited as food, although they could be simply from weeds growing close-by and incorporated incidentally into the sampled deposits. A small number of carrot (*Daucus carota*) seeds were identified in two samples, although again these may represent simply wild plants. Common vegetables would, however, have been an important component of the diet in the medieval period and would have been extensively used, for example, in pottage (Wilson 1991).

The same may also be true for many of the other wild plants represented in the samples from Brayford Pool, now thought of as weeds but previously exploited for food from time to time. For example, the leaves of nettles (*Urtica* spp.), docks (*Rumex* spp.), and goosefoots/oraches (*Chenopodium/Atriplex* spp), may have been picked and added to pottage or eaten as green vegetables. However, these are also common weeds of disturbed ground and waste places, high seed producers, and usually recovered in mixed assemblages, therefore it is virtually impossible to establish whether or not they were actually used as food on the site.

OTHER POTENTIAL USES OF PLANTS

A number of the other plants in the samples may have had various uses; heather (*Calluna vulgaris*) was well represented in a number of samples both as charred and waterlogged remains. Heather has a wide number of potential uses, for example as thatch, fodder, bedding and in wattle and daub walls, as well as a use of fuel, particularly tinder, which would explain the presence of charred remains of heather in several samples. It appears that heather was used as tinder in medieval pottery kilns at Eden Street in Kingston, London (Davis 1999, 16) while documentary evidence shows that it was cut in Sussex for firelighters (Mabey 1996, 159).

Other various uses of wild plants represented in the samples include the sedges (*Carex* spp.) and rushes (*Juncus* spp.), which may have been used as flooring/building materials, while nettles may have been gathered and used for their fibres. A number of potential dye plants were also present including elder and blackberry. Many of the wild plants represented in the samples were also exploited for their medicinal properties; for example, white horehound (*Maribium vulgare*) was used for coughs and lung trouble while black nightshade (*Solanum nigrum*) had great narcotic properties including a use for dropsy (Grieve 1992). However, it is very difficult to differentiate the residues of wild plants gathered and used from those that may have simply been growing locally particularly when the seeds were all found in mixed assemblages as at Brayford Pool.

Wild plants (problems in interpretation)

The vast majority of the botanical remains represented by fruits and seeds in the samples were from wild plants belonging to a range of habitats. There are, however, a number of limitations in the interpretation of this material that need to be highlighted.

Firstly, it is sometimes difficult to categorise all plants by habitat because of the different levels of identification of the material in the samples; thus, plant remains that could only be identified to family or genus cannot provide the same level of ecological information as plants reduced to species because plants within a genus may have significantly different habitats; for instance, the thistles (*Carduus/Cirsium* spp.), hedge parsley (*Torilis* spp.) and stitchworts/chickweeds (*Silene/Stellaria*) species found in a number of samples from the site. This problem may also extend to plants reduced to species level, which are catholic in their habitat requirements, for example sheep's sorrel (*Rumex acetosella*).

Secondly, the importance of different species cannot be valued simply in terms of the number of seeds of each plant found in the samples because of the wide variability in the seed production of individual plants; for instance, weeds of disturbed ground and waste places tend to be high seed producers (eg. goosefoots, nettles) while some wetland plants are also high seed producers such as rushes, which contain between 200,000 and 234,000 seeds per plant. Thus, these may be over-represented in samples while grassland plants, which tend to be low seed producers, may be under-represented.

There are two other taphonomic issues effecting the interpretation of seed assemblages. The first is the differential preservation of fragile as opposed to more robust plant remains, although the generally excellent state of preservation of organic remains in the samples from Brayford Pool probably limits this problem. The second is the various modes of seed dispersal. Seeds may be transported from their original source by wind, water, animals, insects, birds and human activity. It is often difficult, if not impossible, to separate out plant remains representing the residues of imported and used plants, and possibly associated by-products, from plants that may have been either growing on site or close by.

Many of the problems outlined above, however, may be limited by an internal and collective examination of all the plants within an individual assemblage to establish the potential habitat or habitats, while the number of samples in which a species appears rather than individual seed frequency is probably a better way to establish how widespread a plant may have been on site.

Wetland plants

A large number of wetland plants were represented by their fruits and seeds and included aquatic, semi-aquatic and bankside/marshland species. True aquatics were not particularly well represented with just occasional finds in one or two samples of stoneworts (*Chara* spp), duckweed (*Lemna* spp.), pondweed (*Potamogeton* spp.), bulrush (*Schoenoplectus lacustris*) and crowfoots (*Ranunculus batrachium*).

There were a number of bankside/marshland species which also grow in shallow water. Two species that were well represented in the majority of the samples were celery-leaved crowfoot (*Ranunculus sceleratus*) (albeit a high seed producing plant) and bogbean (*Menyanthes trifoliate*). There were also smaller numbers of seeds of water plantain (*Alisma* spp.) in half of the samples and occasional finds of water pepper (*Polygonum hydropiper*), yellow iris (*Iris pseudocarus*) and branched bur-reed (*Sparganium erectum*) in a few samples. Some of the *Apium* species and dropworts (*Oenanthe* spp.), found in several samples are semi-aquatic while nodding bur marigold (*Bidens cernua*) can also grow in water.

Other bankside/marshland species that were well represented and present in most of the samples were rushes, sedges, spike-rush (*Eleocharis palustris/uniglumis*) (all of which, however, are high seed producing plants), and marsh pennywort (*Hydrocotyle vulgaris*), while moderately well represented wetland plants, present in around half the samples, were meadow-rue (*Thalictrum* spp.), gypsywort (*Lycopus europaeus*) and bristle scirpus (*Isolepsis setacea*). Poorly represented in just a few samples, were lesser spearwort (*Ranunculus flammula*), marsh marigold (*Caltha palustris*) and golden dock (*Rumex maritimus*).

Disturbed ground and waste places

There was a wide range of plants of disturbed (including cultivated) ground and waste places, some of which were represented by large numbers of seeds although, as noted above, such weeds are often high seed producers. Nonetheless, it is possible to compare the relative frequency of these different weeds. Some of these plants may have been growing locally while others may have been incidentally imported onto the site as arable weeds together with harvested cereals or through other modes of dispersal.

The best represented weeds of disturbed ground and waste places present in the majority of the samples were corn cockle (*Agrostemma githago*), chickweeds (*Stellaria media* gp), blinks (*Montia fontana*), pale persicaria (*Polygonum lapathifolium*), some of the goosefoots and oraches, stinking mayweed (*Anthemis cotula*, which also appeared as charred seeds) and small nettle (*Urtica urens*). Other weeds, which were not so well represented, were fool's parsley (*Aethusa cynapium*), knotgrass (*Polygonum aviculare*), persicaria (*P. persicaria*), black bindweed (*Fallopia convolvulus*), spiny milk-/sow-thistle (*Sonchus asper*) and possibly some of the docks including sheep's sorrel. There were also a few finds of cornflower (*Centaurea cyanus*), corn salad (*Valerinella dentata*), wild radish (*Raphanus raphanistrum*), field penny-cress (*Thlaspi arvensi*), annual knawel (*Scelaranthus annuus*), hare's ear (*Bupleurum rotundifolium*) and hairy buttercup (*Ranunculus sardous*).

Weeds that are more frequently associated with waste places included the following well represented species in most of the samples; silverweed (*Potentilla anserina*), stinging nettle (*Urtica dioica*), black nightshade, white horehound, nettle leaved goosefoot (*Chenopodium murale*) and glaucous/red goosefoot (*C. glaucum/rubrum*). There were also a few seeds of henbane (*Hyosyamus niger*) and common mallow (*Malva sylvestris*).

A large number of these weeds are closely associated with nutrient rich soils including small and stinging nettle, elder, black nightshade, and some of the goosefoots.

This may be indicative of human activity close-by such as rubbish tips, manure heaps, farmyards etc. Indeed, there are few plants in the samples indicative of nutrient deficient soils with the exception of sheep's sorrel. Some of these weeds are also found exclusively in wet habitats for instance, the blinks, pale persicaria, persicaria, hairy buttercup and silverweed while others are associated with seasonal waterlogging (eg chickweeds, nettles, goosefoots and various *Polygonum* species).

A large number of the weed seeds are also indicators of sandy, acidic and/or loamy soils (eg wild radish, lesser stitchwort, annual knawel, blinks, knotgrass, persicaria, pale persicaria, black bindweed, sheep's sorrel, cornflower, and spiny milk-/sow-thistle). Other plants in the samples are more catholic in their soil requirements, for instance chickweeds and black nightshade, which grow in weakly acid to alkaline soils, while fool's parsley and corn cockle prefer neutral to alkaline loam soils. Other plants, such as stinking mayweed and hare's ear, grow mainly in calcareous loamy clay soils.

This evidence suggests a wide source of the material for the plants represented in the samples; while there is strong evidence for the presence of sandy acidic soils which occur locally, either from plants growing close-by or from plants incidentally imported onto the site as cereal weeds, there is also some evidence for material coming from other soil habitats; this may be a reflection of the different types of soils that were cultivated for cereals.

Shrub/hedgerow plants

Most of these plants were represented by the fruit bearing species discussed above and therefore it is difficult to know if they derive from the residues of consumed food or incidentally from plants growing close-by. Elder seeds were particularly well represented in virtually every sample, hazel nuts and shell fragments in most samples and plum/bullace, sloe/blackthorn, cherry stones and blackberry/raspberry seeds in a small number of samples. There were few other hedgerow/woodland species, with the exception of bryony (*Bryonia dioica*), which was represented in a small number of samples.

Grassland species

There was a range of potential grassland plants although some of the following species are not exclusive to this environment; for example, buttercups (*Ranunculus acris/repens/bulbosus*) which was represented in virtually every sample, may be found in a number of habitats although it has been identified as a characteristic hay meadow plant (Greig 1984). Other potential grassland plants were represented by indeterminate grasses (Poacae), plus occasional finds of seeds of self heal (*Prunella vulgaris*), lesser knapweed (*Centaurea nigra*), hawkbit (*Leontodon* spp.) and sheep's sorrel and possibly some of the sedges and rushes. Small charred grass seeds were found in large numbers in many samples together with some charred brome (*Bromus* spp.) seeds; the latter, however, may have been growing as arable weeds.

Other plants

The remaining plants in the samples (some of which were

well represented) cannot be conveniently divided into one of the above categories either because they could only be identified to genus, for example, thistles (*Carduus/Cirsium* spp.), stitchworts (*Silene* spp.), and violet (*Viola* spp.), or may grow in more than one of these habitats; for example, nipplewort (*Lapsana communis*), which grows in hedges, wood margins, waste places, and hedge parsley (*Torilis* spp.), which is found in hedges, grassy places, and arable fields. Heather was well represented in six samples by both capsules and seeds; this grows on heaths, moors, bogs and open woods on acid soils.

Discussion

An examination of the internal composition of the individual plant assemblages may provide information on the various sources of the material contained within the features.

Ditches
Six samples were taken from ditch fills, these being 112, 128, 185, 187, 156 and 133. The richest plant assemblages in terms of item frequency and species diversity were the samples from 112 and 128, both fills of ditch 191, with the smallest botanical assemblages being in 185, consisting mainly of rootlets, and 156, which contained mostly wood (particularly large amounts of twigs). However, the character of the assemblages were broadly similar, consisting of a mix of mainly wetland and plants of disturbed ground and waste places with varying degrees of evidence for economic plants (mainly in 112 and 128).

Regarding economic plants, all the assemblages contained differing but generally small numbers of charred cereal grains with the largest number being in fills 112 and 128 and just one grain in 156. Small numbers of charred weed seeds, probably from crop cleaning were also present. The samples from 112 and 128 also contained most of the remaining evidence for food/economic plants in the ditch fill samples with very large quantities of very fragmented cereal bran and very large numbers of flax seeds. The presence of bran suggests faecal deposits, which is supported by the insect evidence in these two samples. Smaller amounts of flax seeds and bran were also found in 187.

Sampled fills 112 and 128 also contained virtually all the fruit remains, with occasional stones of plum/bullace, cherry, sloe/blackthorn, shell fragments of hazelnut and large quantities of apple endocarp fragments plus elder and blackberry/raspberry seeds. The last two fruits were also represented in the other samples with large numbers of elder seeds in 185 and particularly in 133. Other potential food residues may be represented by occasional *Brassica/Sinapis* seeds and carrot, the latter found in 128.

A range of wetland plants (aquatic and bankside/marsh-land species) was represented in these samples with seeds of celery-leaved crowfoot, sedges and rushes being particularly abundant. There were few true aquatics, for example stonewort in 156, although there were a number of plants that may be found in standing shallow water, such as celery-leaved crowfoot, bogbean, water dropwort, water plantain and nodding bur marigold.

There were a large number of plants of disturbed ground and waste places including potential arable weeds; for instance, corn cockle fragments were particularly abundant in 112 and 128. Their occurrence, together with large amounts of cereal bran, may represent the residues of the weed being ground up with the cereals and consumed, due to this being a difficult weed seed to remove other than by hand-sorting. Other well represented weeds were chickweeds, nettles, oraches and goosefoots (particularly red/glaucous goosefoot), various *Polygonum* species, black nightshade, blinks (particularly in 133), fool's parsley and stinking mayweed.

Grassland plants in these samples were represented by occasional buttercups, hawkbit, self heal, indeterminate grasses and possibly some of the sedges and rushes, but it would be difficult to use such limited evidence to suggest that the ditches contain the residues of hay fodder and/or stabling materials. On the other hand, large numbers of stem fragments were present in 112, 128 and 187 and less in 156; these included large ribbed hollow stems (both charred and waterlogged in 112) which probably belong to grasses, possibly cereals, and thinner stems in 187; these may represent residues of straw used as bedding or just possibly just the discarded residues of crop-processing.

Heather was represented as charred and waterlogged remains in 112 and 128 and as waterlogged remains in 187; other botanical material included charcoal which was well represented in the ditch fill samples, particularly in fills 128, 133 and 185. These samples also contained large quantities of wood, mosses and occasional other vegetative parts.

Thus, the ditch fill samples contained material from a range of sources. The fills 112, 128 of ditch 191 (and to a lesser extent ditch fill 187) contained most of the residues of human activities; this included evidence of food preparation (grains, fruit stones) and consumption (bran and possibly the fruit and flax seeds), possible hay fodder residues and fuel (charcoal and charred heather, possibly used as tinder). Insect evidence also pointed towards human activity with puparia particularly in large numbers in 112 and smaller amounts in most of the other samples. Beetles analysed from 156 and 187 suggest the presence of decaying settlement matter, which is confirmed by the majority of the weed seeds that grow mainly in nutrient rich soils indicative of rubbish tips and manure heaps. Artefactual debris in the form of pot, marine shell, bone and occasional other material (eg leather in 128 and hammerscale in 133) also points to the occasional dumping of other debris in these ditches.

The presence of Cladoceran ephippia ('water flea' eggs) in all these samples, but particularly in ditch fills 133 and 185, suggests that the ditches would have contained water, possibly being flooded on a periodic or seasonal basis.

Layers
Two samples were taken from layers 106 and 172, neither of which contained particularly rich plant assemblages, either in terms of species diversity or item frequency. There was a predominance of mainly wild plants (weeds of disturbed ground and waste places and some wetland

species) and little evidence for the residues of economic plants.

The few economic plants in the two assemblages consisted of just a small number of charred cereal grains (only one oat grain in 172) plus the residues of wild fruits, many elder seeds, occasional blackberry/raspberry seeds, hazelnut shell and *Prunus* stones. Other potential food residues may be represented by occasional *Brassica/ Sinapis* seeds in 172.

Wetland plants, both aquatic and bankside/marshland species, were present in both samples (although better represented in 106). They included a few true aquatics (eg pondweed in 106), plus semi-aquatic species found in standing shallow water (including celery-leaved crowfoot, bogbean, water plantain and bulrush) and bankside/marshland species (eg rushes, sedges).

There was a relatively wide range of disturbed (including cultivated) ground plants, many of which were indicative of nutrient rich soils and not dissimilar to those weeds recovered from the ditch fill samples; well represented species were the chickweeds, oraches and goosefoots (particularly red/glaucous goosefoot), various *Polygonum* species (particularly pale persicaria in 172), black nightshade, and white horehound (in 106).

There were few grassland plants in the two samples, again mainly represented by sedges and rushes, and a virtual absence of stem fragments. The two samples also contained large quantities of wood, small amounts of charcoal and moss, while 172 contained a large amount of rootlets.

The question was asked as to whether these deposits represent levelling dumps on the margins of Brayford Pool or naturally accumulating foreshore deposits. The quantity of botanical material in the two samples compared to the ditch fill samples may suggest that continuous flooding prevented a more stable plant community developing *in situ*, with the wetland plants, water beetles and Cladoceran ephippia (particularly in 106) and freshwater snails in 172 supporting this interpretation of an aquatic environment. On the other hand, there was some debris associated with human activity, albeit limited, in the form of botanical residues of food preparation (including a little crop-processing debris) and consumption, together with charcoal, plus occasional bone, pot and metal, and large amounts of marine shell in 172. Insect evidence from 172 also points to settlement waste, supported by the good representation of nutrient rich weed species in the two samples. Thus, there appears to have been some dumping of debris, although probably in a haphazard and unplanned way judging by the quantity of remains, while the deposits themselves would have been subjected to flooding, accounting for the aquatic material in the samples and the relatively small plant assemblages in both samples.

Pit fills
Seven pit fills (170, 125, 129, 153, 105, 131 and 127) were analysed and contained variable quantities of generally very well preserved organic remains, with the greatest species diversity being in the sampled pit fills 129, 127 and 131, and the smallest range being in pit fill 170. The

botanical material in each sample was made up of various proportions of the residues of economic (cereals, fruits, flax) and wild plants, mainly wetland species and plants of disturbed (including cultivated) ground and waste places. A few samples also contained some evidence for grassland plants.

Economic plants, mainly food residues, were present in most of the pit fill samples. The richest plant food assemblage was in 131, which contained a very large quantity of fragmented cereal bran, a few cereal grains, a large number of flax seeds and a range of fruits, including sloe/blackthorn and plum bullace stones, hazel nut shell, elder and apple seeds (and a large amount of associated endocarp fragments) and possibly common vegetables (represented by *Brassica/Sinapis* seeds). Sampled pit fills 127 and 129 also contained a few cereal grains, flax (particularly in 129), the residues of fruits (including cherry, apple, endocarp fragments, elder and hazel), and carrot seeds in 129 only. However, most of the pit fill samples produced just a few grains and/or a few wild fruits (elder, blackberry/raspberry and hazel nut shell), for instance in 105, 153 and 170 (elder seeds only). Pit fill 125 contained a larger charred cereal assemblage of almost 50 grains.

A range of wetland species was present in the samples with aquatic, semi aquatic and bankside/marshland species. It was interesting to note that wetland plants were well represented in terms of species diversity and item frequency in the pits from the four earlier fill samples (170, 125, 129 and 153) belonging to Phases 2 and 3; pit fill 170 in particular contained a wide range of mainly wetland plants. These pit fills also contained Cladoceran ephippia, particularly in 153, with aquatic and marsh molluscs in 129. On the other hand, pit fills 105, 131 and 127 from the later Phase 6 produced much less evidence for wetland plants; for instance, pit fill 105 contained virtually no wetland species.

Regarding the range of wetland plants in the pit fill samples, there were relatively few true aquatics, for example stoneworts and duckweed in 125, although some of the semi-aquatic species, celery-leaved crowfoot, bogbean and marsh penywort were particularly well represented, while rushes and sedges were the best represented of the bankside/marshland species.

A wide range of plants of disturbed/cultivated ground and waste places were found in all the samples, particularly in the pit fill samples from Phase 6. The best represented species were corn cockle, chickweeds, stinging and small nettle, oraches and goosefoots (particularly red/glaucous goosefoot), *Polygonum* species (especially persicaria and pale persicaria), stinking mayweed and elder. Silverweed, a plant that grows in waste places, by roadsides, in damp pastures and dunes, was particularly abundant in pit fill 170. These weeds are all characteristic of nutrient rich soils.

There are a number of potential arable weeds, in particular corn cockle, notably abundant in 129 and 131, the latter also containing large quantities of cereal bran (see above), suggesting that the corn cockle seeds may have been accidentally ground up and consumed with the cereals. Stinking mayweed seeds were abundant in 129 and 105, and is a typical weed of calcareous soils, while smaller seed numbers of wild radish (eg in 127 and 105) and cornflower (eg in 129) are both weeds characteristic of sandy acidic soils. Few of the weeds were charred, except for bromes in 125 and very small indeterminate grass seeds in a number of samples.

Potential indicators of grassland and hay meadow habitats were represented by a significantly smaller range of plants, with possible indicators being buttercups, possibly some of the rushes and sedges in most of the samples, and other characteristic hay meadow plants (self heal, hawkbit, thistles, and lesser knapweed in pit fills 105, 127, 129 and 131). However, the abundance of these plants is not great, although as noted above, these are not particularly high seed producers.

Other botanical remains in the pit fill samples included residues of heather in pit fills 127 and 129. Plant stems were present in six of the pit fill samples with the largest amounts being in 127, 131 and 129. Many of these stems were round, ribbed and hollow, suggesting that they may derive from grasses with the very large stems possibly being from cereals. There were, however, also smaller and thinner stems that could be from other plants represented in the samples. A small number of charred hollow stems were present in 129. The stems may represent the residues of hay fodder used as flooring materials (for animals and/or humans), which were later discarded although they could have a more local origin from plants growing close-by. Wood, represented by fragments, shavings and twigs was present in abundant quantities in all the samples, particularly in 153 and 129, with charcoal present in relatively smaller quantities but again in all samples. A few thorns, possibly of hawthorn or sloe, were present in 127. Moss was abundant in 129 and well represented in 127 and 131 with occasional finds in the remaining samples. Rootlets dominated the flot in sampled pit fill 170.

The plant assemblages from the various pit fills examined above show a degree of variation in the potential sources of the material contained within the features and thus the possible use of the different pits. On the one extreme, pit fill 131 has obviously been used for the disposal of the discarded residues of material from food preparation and consumption with the insect evidence (beetles and large amounts of puparia) in addition to the bran fragments indicating faecal deposits in this fill. Insect evidence also pointed to settlement waste in 127 and 129. On the other extreme, the plant remains in pit fill 170 provide little evidence of human activities except for a small quantity of charcoal although all the pit fill samples contained the residues of some pot, marine shell and animal bone from human activities close-by, supported by weeds of nutrient rich soils. The pits may have been subjected to seasonal or periodic flooding, particularly the earlier Phases 2 and 3 pit fill samples.

Slot fill 160
The plant assemblage from this sample produced a wide species diversity which consisted mainly of the residues of economic plants and plants of disturbed (including cultivated) ground and waste places. There were relatively few wetland plants and little evidence for grassland species.

Food plants consisted of large quantities of very fragmented cereal bran, a few charred cereal grains, a very large number of flax seeds and a range of fruits, including sloe/blackthorn and plum/bullace stones, hazel nut shell, blackberry/raspberry seeds and apple/crab apple seeds. The variation in the size of the plum stones in this sample suggests that a number of varieties were represented. A wide range of weeds of disturbed ground and waste places was represented with seeds of corn cockle, chickweeds, goosefoots/oraches and small nettle being particularly abundant, all of which are indicative of nutrient rich soils. The corn cockle fragments probably represent the residues of imported arable weeds ground up and consumed with the processed cereal grain. There were very few wetland plants (eg marsh pennywort) and only occasional semi-aquatic plants (eg bogbean), while potential grassland plants were poorly represented by buttercups, knapweed, hawkbit, thistles, sedges and indeterminate grasses.

Other botanical remains in this sample included very large quantities of wood (bark, twigs, small fragments) and stem fragments, which dominated the flot. The stems were both thick and thin and ribbed, deriving possibly in part from grasses, including cereals. Heather was also fairly well represented along with moss fragments.

This sample has a similar botanical composition to pit fill 131, with a good representation of food plants (preparation and consumption), including evidence for faecal deposits (bran and large amounts of fly puparia). This indicates that it was partially used as a cesspit, although other food residues (bone, a few marine shells) and general waste (eg leather fragments) was also dumped here. The majority of the weed seeds indicate human activities nearby.

Concluding remarks

The analysis of the plant remains from Brayford Pool demonstrated that a wide range of plants was represented in the various sampled features. These included the residues of economic, mainly food plants (including evidence for cess) but also a large quantity of wild plants that appear to have been incorporated into the deposits from both species growing in the vicinity of the sampled features and as part of dumped material.

Residues of human activities were found in most of the samples, particularly in the fills of ditch 191, pit fill 131 and slot fill 160. This suggests deliberate dumping of residues, whereas the quantity of remains in the other samples, particularly the two layers 106 and 172, suggests occasional incidental dumping. As well as the residues of food plants and other artefactual debris, the weed seeds of nutrient rich soils also testify to human habitation close by, with a similar range of weed species frequently occurring in other medieval urban deposits, for example in London. Other wild plants point to the semi-aquatic nature of the local environment with the area appearing to have been subjected to periodic flooding.

Table 6: The plant remains from Phases 1, 2 and 3

		Phase	1	2	2	2	3	3
		Feature	Layer	Ditch 186	Ditch 188	Pit 203	Ditch 191	
		Context	172	185	187	170	112	128
		Vol. of soil (l)	12	22	21	18	30	27
		Flot vol. (ml)	180	300	900	150	1100	800
Latin name	**English**	HAB_USE						
Charred plant remains								
Triticum aestivum L. s.l.	bread/Club Wheat grain	FI		2	1		1	
Triticum sp.	wheat grain	FI					1	
Hordeum sativum L.	barley grain	FI		2	1		4	2
cf. *H. sativum*	?barley grain	FI					2	
cf. *Secale cereale*	?rye grain	FI					1	
Avena sp(p).	oat grain	AFI			2		1	3
cf. *Avena* sp(p).	oat grain	AFI	1	1				4
Cerealia	indet. cereal grain	FI		2	1		11	4
C. vulgaris (L.) Hull	ling/heather capsules	CD					++	++
Anthemis cotula L.	stinking Mayweed	ABGH		1				
Bromus sp(p).	bromes	ABD		1			3	
Poaceae indet.	grass	ABCDEFHI			+		++	+
indeterminate	stem fragments	-					+	+
indeterminate	wood charcoal	-	+++	+++	+++	++	++	+++
Waterlogged plant remains								
Cerealia	indet. cereal bran	FI			+++		++++	++++
cf *Caltha palustris*	?marsh marigold	CE					++	
Ranunculus acris/repens/ bulbosus	buttercups	ABCDEG	++	+	++	+	+	+
R. sardous Crantz	hairy buttercup	ABE	+					
R. flammula L.	lesser spearwort	EG			+			+
R. sceleratus L.	celery-leaved crowfoot	E		+++	+	+++	+	
Thalictrum flavum/minus	meaadow-rue	DE			+	+	+	
Papaver spp.	poppy	ABGHI		+				
Brassica/Sinapis spp.		ABFGHI	+	+	+		+	+
Raphanus raphanistrum L.	wild radish/charlock, siliqua	A						+
Thlaspi arvense L.	field penny-cress	AB					+	
Viola spp.	violet	ABCDG				+		+
Silene spp.	campion/catchfly	ABCDF	+	+	+		+	
Agrostemma githago L.	corn cockle	AB	+		+	+	++++	++++
Stellaria media gp.	chickweeds	ABCDE	++	+++		+	++++	+++
S. graminea type	lesser stitchwort	CD					+	
Stellaria spp.	chickweed/stitchwort	ABCDEG			+			+
Scelaranthus annuus L.	annual knawel	AB						+
Montia fontana ssp. *chondrosperma* L.	blinks	AE	+	+		+		+
Chenopodium murale L.	nettle leaved goosefoot	BD					+	+
C. rubrum/glaucum	red/glaucous goosefoot	AB	+++	+++		+	++	+
Chenopodium spp.	goosefoot Etc.	ABCDFH	+++	+			++	++
Atriplex spp.	orache	ABFGH	+++	+	+	+	++	++

Table 6 (cont.): The plant remains from Phases 1, 2 and 3

		Phase	1	2	2	2	3	3
		Feature	Layer	Ditch 186	Ditch 188	Pit 203	Ditch 191	
		Context	172	185	187	170	112	128
		Vol. of soil (l)	12	22	21	18	30	27
		Flot vol. (ml)	180	300	900	150	1100	800
Latin name	**English**	**HAB_USE**						
Linum usitatissimum L.	cultivated flax	HI			++		+++	++++
Linum spp.	flax	ADHI						++
Rubus fruticosus/idaeus	blackberry/raspberry	CFGH	+				+	
Potentilla anserina L.	silverweed	BDE	++			++++	+	
Potentilla spp.	cinquefoil/tormentil	BCDEFGH	+	+				+
Prunus spinosa L.	sloe/blackthorn	CFG					+	+
P. domestica L.	plum/bullace	CFI					++	+
P. avium type	cherry	CFGI					+	+
Prunus spp.	-	CFGI					+	+
Malus domestica/sylvestris	apple/crab apple	CFHI					+	
M. domestica/sylvestris	apple/crab apple endocarp	CFHI					++++	+++
Pyrus/Malus spp.	pear/apple	CFI						+
Hydrocotyle vulgaris L.	marsh pennywort, white-rot	E	++		+	+++	+	+
Oenanthe spp.	dropwort	DE			+		+	+
Aethusa cynapium L.	fool's parsley	A	+		+		++	+
Torilis spp.	hedge-parsley	ACD	+				+	+
Daucus carota L.	wild carrot	ADFGI						+
Bupleurum rotundifolium L.	hare's-ear	AG					+	
Apium spp.	-	EFI					+	+
Pastinaca sativa L.	wild parsnip	CD					+	+
Umbelliferae indet.	-	-	+				+	+
Bryonia dioica Jacq.	Bryony	CG			++			+
Polygonum aviculare agg	knotgrass	ABG	++		+		++	+
P. persicaria L.	persicaria	ABEH					+	+
P. lapathifolium L.	pale persicaria	ABE	++++			+	+	+
Fallopia convolvulus(L) A. Love	black bindweed	ABF			+			
Polygonum hydropiper/mite	water-pepper	E	+					+
Polygonum spp.	-	ABCDEFG	+				+	+
Rumex acetosella agg.	sheep's sorrel	AD	+					+
Rumex spp.	dock	ABCDEFG	+			+	+	
Rumex spp.	dock perianth	ABCDEFG			+			
Urtica urens L.	small nettle	AB	+	+	++	+++	++++	+++
U. dioica L.	stinging nettle	BCDEFGH	+	+	+	+		+++
Corylus avellana L.	hazel	CF	+		+		+	++
Calluna vulgaris (L.) Hull	ling/heather	CD			++			+
C. vulgaris (L.) Hull	ling/heather capsules	CD					+	+++
Menyanthes trifoliata L.	bogbean	EFG	+		+		+	+
Solanum nigrum L.	black nightshade	BF	++	+	+		++++	++
Mentha spp.	mint	ABCEFGI	+	+				
Lycopus europaeus L.	gipsy-Wort	EH	+		+	++		
Prunella vulgaris L.	self-Heal	BCDG						+

Table 6 (cont.): The plant remains from Phases 1, 2 and 3

		Phase	1	2	2	2	3	3
		Feature	Layer	Ditch 186	Ditch 188	Pit 203	Ditch 191	
		Context	172	185	187	170	112	128
		Vol. of soil (l)	12	22	21	18	30	27
		Flot vol. (ml)	180	300	900	150	1100	800
Latin name	**English**	**HAB_USE**						
Stachys spp.	woundwort	ACEG			+			
Maribium vulgare L.	white horehound	BG		+	+		+	
Labiatae indet	-	-		+				
Sambucus nigra L.	elder	BCFGH	+++	+++	+	+	++	+
Valerianella dentata (L.) Pollich	corn salad	A	+	+				+
Bidens cernua L.	nodding bur marigold	E					++	+
Bidens spp.	bur-marigold	E					+	
Anthemis cotula L.	stinking mayweed	ABGH		+	+		++	+
Carduus/Cirsium spp.	thistles	ABDEG					+	+
Centaurea cyanus L.	cornflower	ABGH					+	
Centaurea spp.	knapweed/thistle	ABDGH			+		++	+
Lapsana communis L.	nipplewort	BCF	+		+		++	++
Leontodon spp.	hawkbit	BDF					+	+
Sonchus asper (L.) Hill	spiny milk-/sow-thistle	AB					+	+
Sonchus spp.	milk-/sow-thistle	ABE						+
Alisma spp.	water plantain	E	+	+		+	+	
Juncus spp.	rush	ADEH	++	++++	++	++++	++	+++
Iris pseudacorus L.	yellow iris, yellow flag	E				+		
Sparganium erectum L.	branched bur-reed	E			+			
Eleocharis palustris/uniglumis	spike-rush	E	+		+		++	++
Isolepis setacea (L.) R.Br.	bristle scirpus	E				++		
Carex spp.	sedge	CDEH	++	++	++	+++	++	++
Carex spp.	sedge uticles	CDEH	+			+++		+
Cypercaeae	sedges etc		++	+	++	+++	++	++
Gramineae indet.	grass	ABCDEFHI				++		++
indeterminate	wood	-	++++	++++	++++	++	+++	++++
indeterminate	stems	-			++++		++++	++++
indeterminate	buds	-					+	++
indeterminate	-	-	+	+	+	+	+	+
Bryophyta indet.	moss	-	+++	++	++	+	++++	++++

(For Key see Table 8)

Table 7: The plant remains from Phases 2, 3, 4 and 5a

		Phase	2	3	3	4	5a
		Feature	Pit 158	Pit 157	Pit 152	Layer	Slot 190
		Context	125	129	153	106	156
		Vol. of soil (l)	23	24	18	22	13
		Flot vol. (ml)	250	400	85	100	400
Latin name	**English**	HAB_USE					
Charred plant remains							
Triticum aestivum L. s.l.	bread/club wheat grain	FI		1		1	
Triticum sp.	wheat grain	FI	1				
Hordeum sativum L.	barley grain	FI	1	3	1		
cf. *H. sativum*	?barley grain	FI	1				
Secale cereale/Triticum sp.	rye/wheat grain	FI	1				
Avena spp.	oat grain	AFI	6				
Avena sativa L.	oat floret grain	AFI		1		1	
cf. *Avena* sp(p).	?oat grain	AFI	8	1	1	2	
Cerealia	indet. cereal grain	FI	32	4		5	1
Vicia/Lathyrus/Pisum sp.	vetch/tare/vetchling/pea	ACDEFI				1	
Anthemis cotula L.	stinking mayweed	ABGH				3	
Bromus spp.	bromes	ABD	5			2	
Poaceae indet.	grass	ABCDEFHI		++++	1		2
indeterminate	stem fragments	-		+			
indeterminate	wood charcoal	-		++	+++	++	++	++
Waterlogged plant remains							
Chara spp.	stonewort	E	+				+
Caltha palustris L.	marsh marigold	CE	+				
Ranunculus acris/repens/ bulbosus	buttercups	ABCDEG		++	++	++	+
R. sardous Crantz	hairy buttercup	ABE		+			+
R. flammula L.	lesser spearwort	EG					+
R. sceleratus L.	celery-leaved crowfoot	E	++++	+	++++	++	
R. Subgen *Batrachium* (DC) A	crowfoots	E		+			
Thalictrum flavum/minus	meadow-rue	DE	+				
Brassica/Sinapis spp.	-	ABFGHI	+				
Raphanus raphanistrum L.	wild radish/charlock , siliqua	A		+			
Viola spp.	violet	ABCDG	+		+	+	+
Hypericum spp.	St John's wort	CDE		+			
Silene spp.	campion/catchfly	ABCDF	+	+		++	
Agrostemma githago L.	corn cockle	AB		+++			
Stellaria media gp.	chickweeds	ABCDE	+	+++	++++	+++	++
S. graminea type	lesser stitchwort	CD	+				
Montia fontana ssp. *chondrosperma* L.	blinks	AE	+		+	+	+
Chenopodium murale L.	nettle leaved goosefoot	BD	+	++		+	
C. rubrum/glaucum	red/glaucous goosefoot	AB	++++	++	+	++	+
Chenopodium spp.	goosefoot Etc.	ABCDFH	++	++	+	++	++
Atriplex spp.	orache	ABFGH	+++	++	++	++	
Linum usitatissimum L.	cultivated flax	HI		+++			
Linum spp.	flax	ADHI		++			+
Rubus fruticosus/idaeus	blackberry/raspberry	CFGH	+				
Potentilla anserina L.	silverweed	BDE	+		++	+	+
Potentilla spp.	cinquefoil/tormentil	BCDEFGH		+	+		+

Table 7 (cont.): The plant remains from Phases 2, 3, 4 and 5a

		Phase	2	3	3	4	5a
		Feature	Pit 158	Pit 157	Pit 152	Layer	Slot 190
		Context	125	129	153	106	156
		Vol. of soil (l)	23	24	18	22	13
		Flot vol. (ml)	250	400	85	100	400
Latin name	**English**	HAB_USE					
Prunus spinosa L.	sloe/blackthorn	CFG					+
P. avium type	cherry	CFGI		+			
Prunus spp.	-	CFGI				+	
Hydrocotyle vulgaris L.	marsh pennywort, white-rot	E	+		++	+	
Oenanthe aquatica/crocata	water dropwort	E		+			
Oenanthe spp.	dropwort	DE	+				+
Aethusa cynapium L.	fool's parsley	A	+	+	+	+	
Bupleurum rotundifolium	hare's-ear	AG		+			
Apium spp.	-	EFI	+				
Torilis spp.	hedge-parsley	ACD		+			
Daucus carota L.	wild carrot	ADFGI		+			
P. persicaria L.	persicaria	ABEH		+			
P. lapathifolium L.	pale persicaria	ABE	+	+++	++		
Umbelliferae indet.	-	-	+	+			
Bryonia dioica Jacq.	Bryony	CG		+			
Polygonum aviculare agg	knotgrass	ABG		+	+	+	
Fallopia convolvulus(L) A. Love	black bindweed	ABF		+	+		
Polygonum spp.	-	ABCDEFG	++	++			
Rumex acetosella agg.	sheep's sorrel	AD			+	+	
R. cf. maritimus	golden dock	DE			+		
Rumex spp.	dock	ABCDEFG	++	+	+	++	
Urtica urens L.	small nettle	AB	++	+++	++++	+	
U. dioica L.	stinging nettle	BCDEFGH		+	+++	+++	
Corylus avellana L.	hazel	CF		+	+		
Calluna vulgaris (L.) Hull	ling/heather	CD		++			
C. vulgaris (L.) Hull	ling/heather capsules	CD		++++			+
Menyanthes trifoliata L.	bogbean	EFG	+++				
Hyoscyamus niger L.	henbane	BDG			+	+	
Solanum nigrum L.	black nightshade	BF	+++	+	+	++	
Lycopus europaeus L.	gipsy-wort	EH	+	+	+		
Lamium cf. *album*	white dead nettle	BC				+	
Lamium sp(p).	dead nettle	ABC			+	+	
Maribium vulgare L.	white horehound	BG		++	+	++	
Labiatae indet	-	-				+	
Sambucus nigra L.	elder	BCFGH	+++	++	+++	+++	++
Anthemis cotula L.	stinking mayweed	ABGH		+++			
Carduus/Cirsium spp.	thistles	ABDEG		+			++
Centaurea cyanus L.	cornflower	ABGH		++			
Centaurea spp.	knapweed/thistle	ABDGH		++			
Leontodon spp.	hawkbit	BDF		+			
Sonchus asper (L.) Hill	spiny milk-/sow-thistle	AB		+			
Sonchus spp.	milk-/sow-thistle	ABE		+			
Compositae	-	-		+			
Alisma spp.	water plantain	E	+		+	++	
Potamogeton spp.	pondweed	E				+	
Juncus spp.	rush	ADEH	++	+++	++++	+++	+++
Sparganium erectum L.	branched bur-reed	E			+		

Table 7 (cont.): The plant remains from Phases 2, 3, 4 and 5a

		Phase	2	3	3	4	5a
		Feature	Pit 158	Pit 157	Pit 152	Layer	Slot 190
		Context	125	129	153	106	156
		Vol. of soil (l)	23	24	18	22	13
		Flot vol. (ml)	250	400	85	100	400
Latin name	**English**	**HAB_USE**					
Lemna spp.	duckweed	E	+				
Eleocharis palustris/uniglumis	spike-Rush	E		+			
Schoenoplectus lacustris (L.) Palla	bulrush	E				+	
Isolepis setacea (L.) R.Br.	bristle scirpus	E	++	+	+	++	
Carex spp.	sedge	CDEH	++	+++	+++	+++	+
Carex spp.	sedge uticles	CDEH		++	++		
Cypercaeae	sedges etc	-	+++	++	+	++	++
Poaceae indet.	grass	ABCDEFHI	+	+			
indeterminate	wood	-	++++	+++++	++++	++	++++
indeterminate	stems	-	++	+++	+		++
indeterminate	buds	-		++			
indeterminate	-	-	+		+	+	+
Bryophyta indet.	moss	-	+	++++	++	+	++

(For Key see Table 8)

Table 8: The plant remains from Phases 5b and 6

		Phase	5b	5b	5b	6	6
		Feature	Pit 144	Pit 139	Pit 146	Ditch 143	Slot 140
		Context	131	105	127	133	160
		Vol. of soil (l)	24	24	20	20	11
		Flot vol. (ml)	800	1000	500	180	500
Latin name	**English**	**HAB_USE**					
Charred plant remains							
Triticum aestivum L. s.l.	bread/club wheat grain	FI	1				
Triticum spp.	wheat grain	FI				2	
Hordeum sativum L.	barley grain	FI	1			1	3
cf. *H. sativum*	?barley grain	FI				2	
Hordeum/Triticum sp	barley/wheat grain	FI			1		
Avena spp.	oat grain	AFI		2			
cf. *Avena* sp(p).	?oat grain	AFI			1	2	1
Cerealia	indet. cereal grain	FI	2	2	5	5	1
Poaceae indet.	grass	ABCDEFHI	++	++	++	+	+
indeterminate	wood charcoal	-	++	+++	++	+++	+++
Waterlogged plant remains							
Cerealia	indet. cereal bran	FI	++++				++++
Ranunculus acris/repens/bulbosus	buttercups	ABCDEG	+	+	+	+	+
R. sardous Crantz	hairy buttercup	ABE		+	+	+	
R. parviflorus L.	small-flowered buttercup	CD		+			

Table 8 (cont.): The plant remains from Phases 5b and 6

		Phase	5b	5b	5b	6	6
		Feature	Pit	Pit	Pit	Ditch	Slot
			144	139	146	143	140
		Context	131	105	127	133	160
		Vol. of soil (l)	24	24	20	20	11
		Flot vol. (ml)	800	1000	500	180	500
Latin name	**English**	**HAB_USE**					
R. sceleratus L.	celery-leaved crowfoot	E				+	+++
Thalictrum flavum/minus	meadow-rue	DE	+	+		+	
Brassica/Sinapis spp.	-	ABFGHI				+	
Raphanus raphanistrum L.	wild radish/charlock , siliqua	A		++	++		
Thlaspi arvense L.	field penny-cress	AB		+			
Viola spp.	violet	ABCDG	+		+		
Hypericum spp.	St John's wort	CDE				+	
Silene spp.	campion/catchfly	ABCDF		+++		++	
Lychnis flos-cuculi L.	ragged robin	CDE	+				
Agrostemma githago L.	corn cockle	AB	+++		+		++++
Stellaria media gp.	chickweeds	ABCDE	+++	++	++++	++	++++
Stellaria spp.	chickweed/stitchwort	ABCDEG		++			
Scleranthus annuus L.	annual knawel	AB	+				+
Montia fontana ssp. chondrosperma L.	blinks	AE	+	+	+	+++	
Chenopodium murale L.	nettle leaved goosefoot	BD				+	
C. rubrum/glaucum	red/glaucous goosefoot	AB	+	+	++	++++	+
Chenopodium spp.	goosefoot etc.	ABCDFH	+	+	++	++	++
Atriplex spp.	orache	ABFGH	++	+++	++	++	++
Malva sylvestris L.	mallow	BF	+				+
Linum usitatissimum L.	cultivated flax	HI	+++		+		++++
Linum spp.	flax	ADHI			+		++
Rubus fruticosus/idaeus	blackberry/raspberry	CFGH				+	+
Potentilla anserina L.	silverweed	BDE	+	+	+	++	+
Potentilla spp.	cinquefoil/tormentil	BCDEFGH	+	+			
Prunus spinosa L.	sloe/blackthorn	CFG	+				+
P. domestica L.	plum/bullace	CFI	+				+
Prunus spp.	-	CFGI					+
Malus domestica/sylvestris	apple/crab apple	CFHI	+		+		++
M. domestica/sylvestris	apple/crab apple endocarp	CFHI	+++		++++		
Pyrus/Malus spp.	pear/apple	CFI					+
Hydrocotyle vulgaris L.	marsh pennywort, white-rot	E	+			+	++
Oenanthe spp.	dropwort	DE	+				
Aethusa cynapium L.	fool's parsley	A		++	+	+	+
Bupleurum rotundifolium L.	hare's-ear	AG		++	+		
Apium spp.	-	EFI	+			+	
Torilis spp.	hedge-parsley	ACD		++			
Umbelliferae indet.	-	-	+	++	+	+	+
Bryonia dioica Jacq.	Bryony	CG				+	
Polygonum spp.	-	ABCDEFG		++			+
Polygonum aviculare agg	knotgrass	ABG		+	+		+
P. persicaria L.	persicaria	ABEH		+++			
P. lapathifolium L.	pale persicaria	ABE	+	+	+		++
Fallopia convolvulus(L) A. Love	black bindweed	ABF	+		++		+
Rumex spp.	dock	ABCDEFG	+	++	+		+
Urtica urens L.	small Nettle	AB	+++		++	+	++++
U. dioica L.	stinging Nettle	BCDEFGH				++	+

Table 8 (cont.): The plant remains from Phases 5b and 6

		Phase	5b	5b	5b	6	6
		Feature	Pit 144	Pit 139	Pit 146	Ditch 143	Slot 140
		Context	131	105	127	133	160
		Vol. of soil (l)	24	24	20	20	11
		Flot vol. (ml)	800	1000	500	180	500
Latin name	**English**	HAB_USE					
Corylus avellana L.	hazel	CF	+		+		+
Calluna vulgaris (L.) Hull	ling/heather	CD			++++		++
C. vulgaris (L.) Hull	ling/heather capsules	CD			++++		++
Menyanthes trifoliata L.	bogbean	EFG	+		+	+	+
Solanum nigrum L.	black nightshade	BF				+++	++
Lycopus europaeus L.	gipsy-wort	EH				+	
Prunella vulgaris L.	self-heal	BCDG	+		+		
Maribium vulgare L.	white horehound	BG	+	++	+	+	++
Labiatae indet	-	-	+			++	+
Sambucus nigra L.	elder	BCFGH	+	++	++	++++	
Valerianella dentata (L.) Pollich	corn salad	A		+	+		
Anthemis cotula L.	stinking mayweed	ABGH	+	+++	+		++
Carduus/Cirsium spp.	thistles	ABDEG		+++	+		+
Centaurea cyanus L.	cornflower	ABGH					+
C. cf *cyanus*	?cornflower	ABGH	+	+			
C. nigra L.	lesser knapweed	BDG		+			
C. cf. *nigra*	?lesser knapweed	BDG			+		
Centaurea spp.	knapweed/thistle	ABDGH	+	++	++		++
Lapsana communis L.	nipplewort	BCF	+	++	++		
Leontodon spp.	hawkbit	BDF		+			+
Picris echioides L.	bristly ox-tongue	BC					+
Sonchus asper (L.) Hill	spiny milk-/sow-thistle	AB	+		++		++
Sonchus spp.	milk-/sow-thistle	ABE			+		+
Alisma spp.	water plantain	E				+	
Juncus spp.	rush	ADEH			+++	+++	
Iris pseudacorus L.	yellow iris, yellow flag	E				+	
Sparganium erectum L.	branched bur-reed	E	+				
Eleocharis palustris/uniglumis	spike-rush	E	+	+	+		+
Isolepis setacea (L.) R.Br.	bristle scirpus	E				+	
Scirpus spp.	club rush	E				+	
Carex spp.	sedge	CDEH	++	+	++	++	+
Cypercaeae	sedges etc		+	++	+	+++	+
Poaceae indet.	grass	ABCDEFHI	+		+		+
indeterminate	wood	-	++++	+++++	++++	++++	++++
indeterminate	stems	-	++++	++	++++		++++
indeterminate	buds	-	+		++		+
indeterminate	-	-	+	+	+	+	+
Bryophyta indet.	moss	-	+++	+	+++		++

Key:
habitat and use codes: A = weeds of cultivated land; B = weeds of waste places and disturbed ground;
C= plants of woods, scrub, hedgerows; D = open environments (fairly undisturbed);
E= plants of damp/wet environments; F = edible plants; G = medicinal and poisonous plants;
H= commercial/industrial use; I = cultivated plants
Frequency: + = 1-10 items; ++ =11-50 items; +++ = 51-150 items; ++++ = 150= items

Insect remains
by David Smith and Michelle Morris

Introduction

Insect faunas from eleven of the soil samples were analysed in order to help answer a number of specific questions concerning the archaeology of the site:

1   some samples were believed to have developed as part of the strand line of the Pool or flood debris. Is there evidence for this in the insects present?

2   the deposits were divided into three descriptive categories during assessment by The Environmental Archaeological Consultancy (Rackham 2001). These consisted of mineral rich deposits, organic deposits and apparent cess pit fills. It was hoped that an examination of the insect remains might allow the nature of the deposits present to be identified or confirmed.

Sample processing and analysis

The samples were processed using the standard method of paraffin flotation as outlined in Kenward *et al* (1980). The insect remains present were sorted from the flots and stored in ethanol. The Coleoptera (beetles) present were identified by direct comparison to the Gorham and Girling Collections of British Coleoptera. The various taxa of insects recovered from these samples are presented in Table 9. The context and feature numbers relating to the samples are given in Table 4. The taxonomy follows that of Lucht (1987). The number of individuals and number of species present in each sample are outlined in Table 9 and Figure 13.

Where applicable each species of Coleoptera has been assigned to one or more ecological groupings and these are indicated in the second column of Table 9. These groupings are derived from the preliminary classifications outlined by Kenward (1978). The classification used here follow that used in Kenward and Hall (1995). The groupings themselves are described at the end of Table 9. The various proportions of these groups, expressed as percentages of the total Coleoptera present in the faunas, are shown in Table 10 and Figure 14.

Some of the Coleoptera have also been assigned codes based upon their extent of synanthropy. This includes the proportions of Kenward's (Hall and Kenward 1990; Kenward and Hall 1995) 'house fauna' (species apparently particularly associated with human settlements) and those with known synanthropic preferences. These codes are derived from those used by Kenward (1997). The synanthropic groupings are described at the end of Table 9 and the individual codes for the relevant species are shown in column 3 of Table 9. The proportions of these synanthropic groupings, expressed as a percentage of the total fauna, is presented in Table 11 and Figure 15.

The dipterous (fly) puparia were identified using Smith (1973, 1989) and, where possible, by direct comparison to specimens identified by Skidmore (1999). The taxonomy follows that of Smith (1989) for the Diptera.

Mineral-rich deposits

Only two of the faunas examined, deriving from layer 172 and ditch fill 185, came from this type of deposit. Both contexts produced very small amounts of insect remains (Table 12 and Figure 13). The limited size of both faunas suggests that they may not be representative of the deposit.

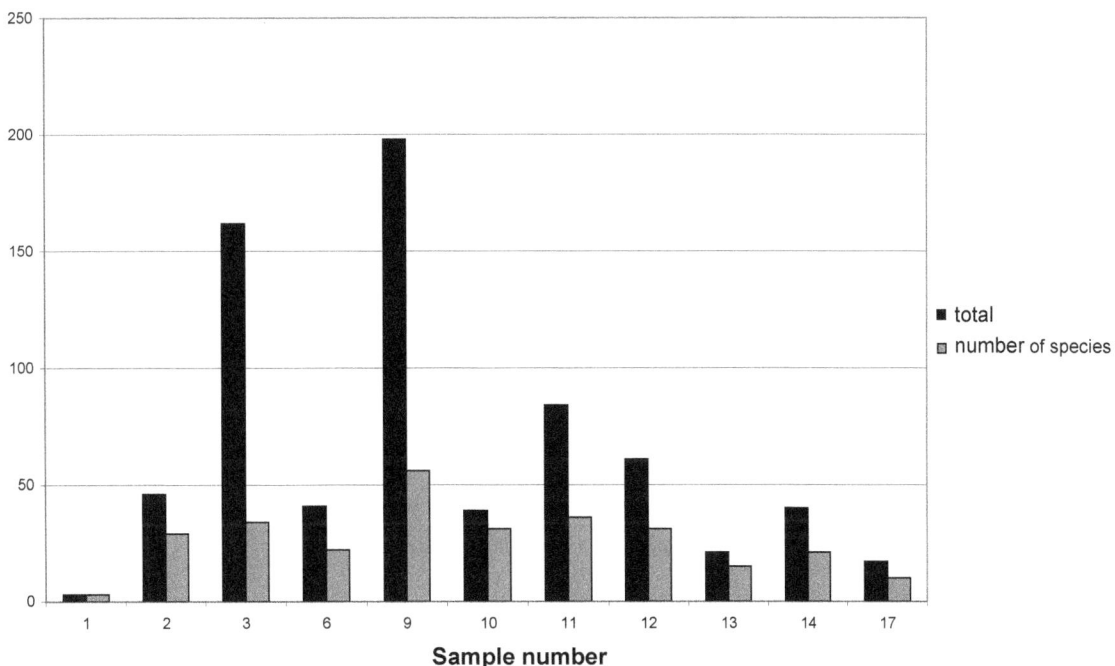

Fig 13: The total number of individuals and species for the insect faunas

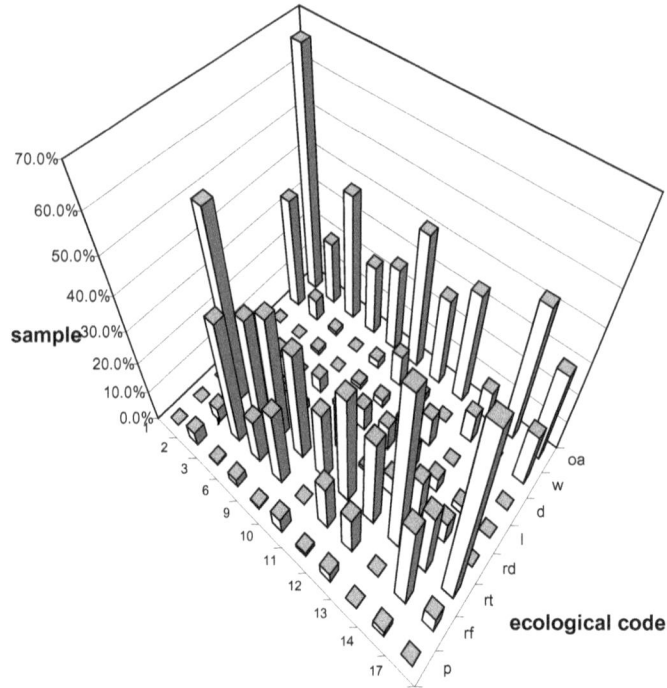

Fig 14: The proportions of ecological groupings in the samples

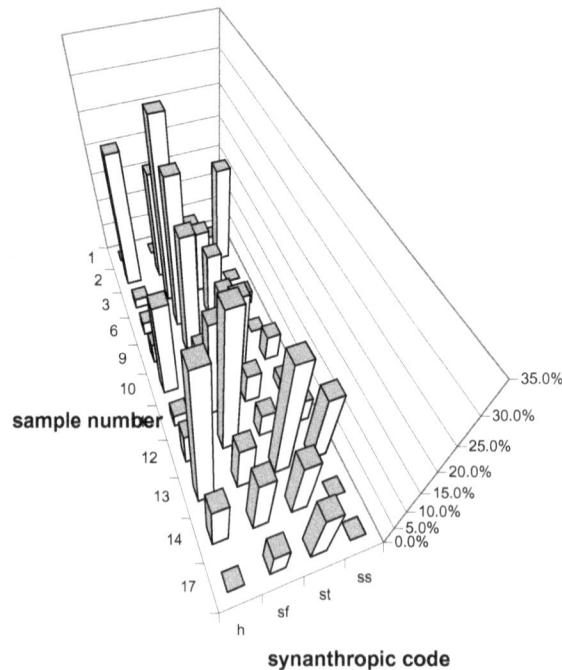

Fig 15: The proportions of synanthropic groupings in the samples

However, the species contained in both samples are commonly associated with a wide range of decaying material and settlement wastes in the archaeological record. This includes taxa that belong to ecological groupings "rd" and "rt" in Table 10 and Figure 14. Examples of this grouping are the *Omalium*, *Xylodromus concinnus* and *Neobisnius* species of Rove beetle. Equally, the limited fauna of Cryptophagidae and Lathridiidae encountered suggests the presence of drier but still mouldering, organic matter. The presence of settlement waste is also indicated by the two pupae of the common housefly (*Musca domestica*), a species which today is still associated with household rubbish (Smith 1989).

A small fauna of water beetles is present, including species such as *Agabus* and *Hydroporus* that may be derived from the nearby Pool during times of flood. Unfortunately, if these contexts represented land surfaces, this is not reflected in the insect faunas examined. None of the many possible species of beetle, which are associated with undergrowth, Poolside vegetation or grassy areas, were encountered here.

In summary, the small faunas of insects recovered from these mineral rich deposits suggest that the deposit incorporated settlement waste and, perhaps, some flood deposit material.

Organic deposits

Insect faunas were analysed from four samples from contexts identified as organic deposits.

In the sample taken from ditch fill 156, the vast majority of species present are associated with settlement waste in the archaeological record. In terms of the beetles present this aspect of the fauna contains numbers of small rove beetles such as *Xylodromus concinnus*, *Neobisnius* and *Falagria*. The latter two of these species are probably associated with rather foul deposits. Once again Lathridiidae and Cryptophagidae species suggest the incorporation of drier material. The origin of this material as settlement waste is strongly indicated by the presence of a number of species that are closely associated with human housing and other buildings. This is particularly the case with a large tenebrionid or darkling beetle (*Tenebrio obscurus*), which Kenward (Kenward 1997) has suggested is associated with long-term settlements and probably with housing. Another species commonly found in these faunas is the woodworm (*Anobium punctatum*) which is a common pest of structural timbers.

Three of the samples came from pits (pit fills 129, 127 and 187). The insect faunas present in these fills are dominated by species associated with decaying settlement waste (represented by the high percentages of ecological groupings associated with rotting and foul material (ecological groupings rt and rf in Table 10 and Figure 14). This element of the fauna includes many of the same taxa as seen in gully fill 156, but also includes large numbers of species such as the *Aphodius* dung beetles and *Cercyon*. These taxa are associated with very rotten and foul material. The interpretation of three dung beetles can be initially misleading. However, the species present do not necessarily indicate the inclusion of animal dung in the context. The three taxa encountered, *Aphodius prodromus/sphacelatus*, *A. fimentarius* and *A. granarius* are amongst the most ecological unspecific of the dung beetles. They are found in a variety of rotting material, as well as herbivore dung (Jessop 1986). In addition, they are common inhabitants of archaeological settlements, where they appear to be associated with rather fluid and foul wastes (Kenward and Hall 1995, Carrott and Kenward 2001).

The small fauna of flies recovered from these deposits also suggests the presence of fairly rotten material. *Stomoxys calcitrans*, recovered from pit fill 129, is the stable or biting housefly, which commonly occurs in either cow dung or fluid settlement wastes (Smith 1989). Calaphorid larvae, found in ditch fill 187, are the common bluebottles and are normally associated with decaying substances, particularly carrion (Smith 1989). The larvae of the Sepsis flies also commonly breed in dung and excrement (Smith 1989).

All these contexts contain a relatively small fauna of ground beetles and plant feeding species, mainly leaf beetles and weevils, which are commonly associated with open and vegetated ground. None of the species encountered would be out of place in the open and waste areas of settlements. These taxa are represented as ecological groupings "oa" and "p" in Tables 9 and 10 and Figure 13. Certainly, it is clear from these statistics that these three contexts contain the highest proportions of these groupings from all of the samples examined at this site. This may suggest that these features remained open for some time. Given this, and the comparative lack of beetles associated with bodies of water, this may suggest that the Pool did not flood substantially during the time of the deposition of material in this area of the site.

Cess pits and cess rich deposits

Four of the samples examined here are thought to have an origin as faecal waste deposits. These are the fills of ditch 191 (112 and 128) and pit fills 116 and 131.

The species of fly recovered strongly indicate this is the case. The very large numbers of Sepsis flies are probably particularly indicative of the presence of faecal matter (Smith 1989). The same is true of *Thoracochaeta zostera*. Skidmore (1999) suggests that this species is typical of archaeological cesspits. Today, it is only found in accumulations of seaweed at the high water mark (Skidmore 1999). Belshaw (1989) holds that its presence probably indicates that the consistency of archaeological cesspits, filled with faecal material and water containing high concentrations of dissolved substances, probably had much in common with decaying seaweed. Sarcophaga flies are also commonly associated with faecal material. The large numbers of parasite ova also recorded from these contexts by John Carrott supports this conclusion.

Other flies and beetles may have had an origin in settlement waste and rubbish dumped in with the cess. This is clearly indicated by a number of species of beetle that Kenward (1997) holds have a particularly strong association with human settlement, and which he describes as being strongly synanthropic. These are the ground beetle *Pristonychus terricola*, the colydid *Aglenus brunneus* and the two species of darkling beetle, *Blaps mucronata* and *Tenbrio molitor*. The relatively large numbers of Kenward's "house fauna" and the synanthropic species present (Table 11 and Figure 14) also suggest an origin in housing or settlement materials.

Amongst the beetles there are also a relatively high proportion of species associated with very rotten material (ecological grouping "rt" in Table 10 and Figure 14). In particular, this includes various *Cercyon* species, the histerid pill beetles, such as *Parlister pupurascens*

Table 9: The insect remains

Sample	Eco	Syn	1	2	3	6	9	10	11	12	13	14	17
Context			105	156	160	129	131	127	112	128	185	187	172
COLEOPTERA													
Carabidae													
Carabus granulatus L.	oa		-	-	-	-	1	-	-	-	-	-	-
Clivina fossor (L.)	oa		-	-	1	1	-	1	1	1	-	1	1
Dyschirus globosus (Hbst.)	oa		-	1	-	-	-	-	1	-	-	-	-
Bembidion spp.	oa		-	1	-	-	1	-	1	-	-	-	1
Anisodactylus binotatus (F.)	u		-	-	-	-	-	1	-	-	-	-	-
Pterostichus nigrita (Payk.)	oa		-	-	-	-	-	-	-	1	-	-	-
P. melanarius (Ill.)	oa		1	-	-	1	1	2	1	1	-	1	-
P. madidus (F.)	oa		-	-	-	-	1	-	-	-	-	-	-
Pristonychus terricola (Hbst.)	u	ss	-	-	-	-	-	-	1	1	1	-	-
Amara spp.	oa		-	-	1	-	1	-	-	1	-	-	-
Dytiscidae													
Hydrophorus spp.	oa-w		-	-	1	-	-	1	-	-	-	-	-
Agabus spp.	oa-w		-	-	-	-	1	-	-	-	-	-	2
Colymbetes fuscus (L.)	oa-w		-	1	-	-	-	-	-	-	-	-	-
Hydraenidae													
Ochthebius spp.	oa-w		1	1	-	-	1	-	-	-	-	-	-
Helophorus spp.	oa-w		-	1	-	-	-	1	1	-	1	-	-
Hydrophilidae													
Coalostoma orbiculare (F.)	oa-w		-	-	-	-	-	-	-	-	1	-	1
Sphaeridium lunatum F.	rf	sf	-	-	3	-	1	-	-	-	-	-	-
Cercyon impressus (Sturm)	rf	sf	-	-	2	-	17	-	-	-	-	1	-
C. unipuntatus (L.)	rf	st	-	-	2	-	-	-	1	-	-	-	1
C. atricapillus (Marsh.)	rf	st	-	-	7	-	-	-	3	-	-	-	-
C. analis (Payk.)	rt	sf	-	1	40	5	5	-	-	5	-	1	-
C. spp.	rt		-	-	-	-	18	-	10	-	-	-	-
Megasternum boletophagum (Marsh.)	rt		-	-	-	-	1	-	-	-	-	-	-
Hydrobius fusipes (L.)	oa-w		-	-	-	-	-	1	-	-	-	-	-
Laccobius sp.	oa-w		-	-	-	-	-	-	1	-	-	-	-
Histeridae													
Acritus nigricornis (Hoffm.)	rt	st	-	-	1	-	1	-	-	-	-	-	-
Gnathoncus spp.			-	2	-	-	1	-	-	-	-	-	-
Grammostethus marginatus (Er.)	rt	sf	-	-	-	-	-	-	1	-	-	-	-
Paralister purpurascens (Hbst.)	rt	sf	-	-	1	-	1	-	-	-	-	-	-
Hister cadaverinus Hoffm.	rt	sf	-	-	1	1	3	-	2	4	-	-	1
Catopidae													
Catops spp.			-	-	-	-	1	-	1	-	-	-	-

Table 9 (cont.): The insect remains

Sample no. Context no.	Eco	Syn	1 105	2 156	3 160	6 129	9 131	10 127	11 112	12 128	13 185	14 187	17 172
Ptiliidae													
Ptilidae Genus & spp. indet.	rt		-	3	-	-	2	-	-	-	-	-	-
Staphylinidae													
Omalium riparium Thoms.	rt	sf	-	-	-	-	3	-	-	-	-	-	-
O. rivulare (Payk.)	rt	sf	-	-	-	-	-	-	1	-	-	-	-
O. spp.	rt		-	-	-	-	-	-	2	1	1	-	-
Xylodromus concinnus (Marsh.)	rt-h	st	-	1	-	-	1	1	-	-	2	-	-
Acidota crenata (F.)	oa		-	-	-	-	-	1	-	-	-	-	-
Trogophloeus bilineatus (Steph.)	rt	sf	-	-	1	-	2	-	-	1	-	-	-
T. spp.	u		-	1	1	-	-	-	-	-	-	1	1
Oxytelus sculptus Grav.	rt	st	-	-	4	-	10	-	1	-	-	-	-
Oxytelus rugosus (F.)	rt		-	-	1	1	3	1	2	1	1	-	1
O. scupturatus Grav.	rt		-	-	-	-	1	-	1	-	-	1	-
O. nitidulus Grav.	rt-d		-	-	-	-	2	1	-	-	-	-	-
O. tetracarinatus (Block)	rt	sf	-	-	-	1	-	-	1	-	-	1	-
Platystethus arenarius (Fourc.)	rf		-	1	9	-	1	-	1	1	-	1	-
P. corntus (Grav.)	oa-d		-	-	-	-	-	-	-	-	-	4	-
Stenus spp.	u		-	1	1	-	1	1	-	-	1	1	-
Lathrobium spp.	oa		-	-	2	1	-	-	-	-	-	-	-
Leptracinus spp.	rt	st	-	-	-	-	1	-	-	-	-	-	-
Gyrohypnus fracticornis (Müll.)	rt	st	-	-	2	4	1	-	-	1	-	2	1
Xantholinus spp.			-	1	-	1	1	1	-	2	-	1	-

Ecological coding (Kenward and Hall 1995)
oa (& ob) - Species which will not breed in human housing.
w- aquatic species.
d- species associated with damp watersides and river banks.
rd- species primarily associated with drier organic matter.
rf - species primarily associated with foul organic matter, often dung.
rt - insects associated with decaying organic matter but not belonging to either the rd or rf groups.
l - species associated with timber.
h - members of the 'house fauna' this is a very arbitrary group based on archaeological associations (Hall and Kenward 1990).

Synanthropic codings (Kenward 1997).
sf - faculative synanthropes, common in 'natural' habitats but clearly favoured by artificial ones.
st - typically synanthropes, particularly favoured by artificial habitats but believed to be able to survive in nature in the long term.
ss - strong synanthropes, essentially dependant on human activity for survival.

Table 10: The proportion of ecological groupings present in the samples

Sample	1	2	3	6	9	10	11	12	13	14	17
oa	66.7%	19.6%	38.2%	22.0%	26.3%	41.0%	27.4%	34.4%	9.5%	42.5%	29.4%
w	33.3%	6.5%	1.2%	0.0%	2.5%	10.3%	2.4%	0.0%	9.5%	0.0%	17.6%
d	0.0%	0.0%	1.2%	0.0%	1.5%	2.6%	1.2%	9.8%	0.0%	10.0%	0.0%
l	0.0%	2.2%	0.0%	4.9%	1.5%	7.7%	8.3%	8.2%	4.8%	2.5%	0.0%
rd	0.0%	6.5%	3.1%	2.4%	3.5%	15.4%	1.2%	6.6%	14.3%	7.5%	0.0%
rt	0.0%	56.5%	32.7%	39.0%	34.8%	23.1%	35.7%	29.5%	52.4%	22.5%	58.8%
rf	0.0%	4.3%	38.8%	14.6%	24.2%	0.0%	15.4%	13.1%	0.0%	30.0%	5.9%
p	0.0%	4.3%	0.6%	2.4%	0.5%	5.1%	1.2%	3.3%	0.0%	2.5%	0.0%

Table 11: The proportions of synanthropic groupings present in the samples

Sample	1	2	3	6	9	10	11	12	13	14	17
h	0.0%	23.9%	1.8%	2.4%	4.0%	17.9%	2.4%	6.6%	28.6%	10.0%	0.0%
sf	0.0%	19.6%	31.5%	26.8%	22.2%	7.7%	19.0%	27.9%	9.5%	12.5%	5.9%
st	0.0%	8.7%	11.7%	12.2%	10.6%	15.4%	6.0%	4.9%	23.8%	12.5%	11.8%
ss	0.0%	17.4%	0.0%	2.4%	0.0%	5.1%	2.4%	4.9%	14.3%	0.0%	0.0%

and *Hister cadaverinus*, and the *Aphodius* dung beetles already mentioned. Similar material is also probably inhabited by several of the rove beetles present such as the various *Oxytelus* and *Omalium* species. It is also possible that the *Philonthus*, unfortunately not identifiable to species level, may inhabit a similar environment. There has recently been an argument over the specific origin of faunas associated with very rotten material in cesspits. Osborne (1983) holds that they are inhabitants of the cesspit itself whereas Kenward (pers com) prefers to see them as incorporated into cesspits as part of rubbish disposal. However, the author (DNS) has found this group of species of beetles often occurs in deposits identified as cesspits from a number of sites in medieval London.

One species worthy of particular comment, coming from the fill of beam slot 140 (fill 160), is the *Bruchus pisorum*, of which 12 individuals were present. This species is a field pest of peas and beans. It often hatches as adults in store. It may be that spoiled pulses were dumped into the pits. Equally, these individuals may have been consumed by humans and entered the cesspit along a similar route to that outlined by Osborne (1983) for the grain pests, since no pulses were recognised in this sample.

The presence of rather rotten settlement waste is also indicated by the remaining species of flies present. The

occurrence of *Callipora* again indicates the presence of decaying carrion, as possibly does *Hydrotaea* ?*dentipes* (Smith 1989). The remaining Muscidae, such as *Musca domestica* (the common house fly), *Muscina stabulans* (the lesser house fly) and *Stomoyxs calcitrans* are all associated with decaying organic wastes and rubbish.

There are a small proportion of beetles (ecological groups "oa" and "p"), usually ground beetles or weevils, which appear to be from more open areas of ground and grassland. It is probable that these have entered the pits from the landsurface around them rather than through the introduction of material such as hay (an example of this process can be seen in Kenward and Hall 1997).

Equally, there is a small fauna of beetles that are associated with aquatic environments (ecological groups "w" and "d"). This includes small numbers of water beetles such as *Agabus*, *Hydroporus*, *Octhebius* and *Helophorus*. A number of the weevils recovered are associated with specific species of aquatic plants. *Notaris acridulus* is normally associated with *Glyceria flutans* (the flote-grass) and *Tanysphyrus lemnae* with *Lemna* species (duckweeds). Taken together both of these groups of taxa would appear to indicate that there is a possibility that these pits may have been seasonally flooded.

Table 12: The total numbers of individuals and species for the insect faunas

Sample	1	2	3	6	9	10	11	12	13	14	17
Context	105	156	160	129	131	127	112	128	185	187	172
Total	3	46	162	41	198	39	84	61	21	40	17
Number of species	3	29	34	22	56	31	36	31	15	21	10

Conclusions and comparisons

It is clear from the beetles and flies present that considerable amounts of settlement and human waste were incorporated into these deposits as they accumulated. Given that much of this material occurs in pits it is probable that this deposition was deliberate. There is slight evidence that these deposits may have been flooded periodically.

The insect fauna recorded from these early medieval deposits are typical of large human archaeological settlements of this period. An essentially similar range of species were present in the urban materials and rubbish spreads at Anglo-Scandinavian York (Kenward and Hall 1995), medieval Beverley (Hall and Kenward 1980), Anglo-Norman Durham (Kenward 1979), late medieval Stone (Moffett and Smith 1997) and a range of sites from Saxon and medieval London (Smith 1995, 1998, 1999, 2001; Smith and Chandler 1995). In terms of dipterous faunas associated with archaeological cesspits, the Lincoln faunas are very similar to those at medieval Bull Wharf (Smith 1998), Preacher's Court (Smith 1999) and One Poultry (Smith 2001).

Charcoal and waterlogged wood
by Rowena Gale

Introduction

Waterlogging in pits and ditches ensured the preservation of wood and charcoal deposits. Waterlogged wood was abundant in all samples and usually consisted of roundwood (with bark *in situ*), fragments (chips/slivers) from large wood and loose bark from wide roundwood, poles/trunkwood. Most of the roundwood was soft and degraded and many pieces had become partially mineralised through the deposition of extraneous deposits - the anatomical examination of mineralised fragments was extremely difficult or, in most instances, impossible. Wood chips and slivers from large wood were better preserved. Tool marks were displayed on some fragments. Charcoal occurred in most contexts, although in much smaller quantities, with the exception of deposit 211 which contained abundant quantities of firm, well-preserved charcoal fragments.

The wood remains seem to have derived mainly from dumped domestic fuel debris, artefactual materials, wood-working waste and the accumulated debris from surrounding woody vegetation.

Eleven samples (10 wood and 1 charcoal) were selected for detailed study from pits and ditches relating to Phases 2, 3, 5 6, and 7. The single charcoal sample (deposit 211) examined was associated with hammerscale and slag.

The analysis was undertaken to:

i) clarify the origins of the wood and charcoal
ii) to assess the use of the roundwood for purposes other than as fuel
iii) determine whether domestic fuel differed from industrial fuel
iv) indicate whether fuel was gathered from managed woodland or other sources
v) assess the character of woodland management
vi) identify the wood used for a carved wooden artefact from the fill (160) of slot 140.

Materials and methods

In view of the large quantity of material and to keep within budget a representative number of fragments was examined from all samples. For waterlogged wood this included a range of stem diameters from the narrowest possible (2mm) to the widest – although, in reality, selection was often restricted by the poor condition of the roundwood; large wood fragments were examined in full. Approximately 70% of the charcoal was examined.

Samples were prepared for examination using standard methods (Gale and Cutler 2000). Thin sections of waterlogged wood were mounted on microscope slides and examined using transmitted light on a Nikon Labophot-2 microscope at magnifications up to x400. Charcoal fragments were supported in washed sand and examined using incident light on the same microscope. The anatomical structures were matched to prepared reference slides. When possible, the maturity of the wood was assessed (ie heartwood/sapwood), and stem diameters and the number of growth rings recorded.

The roundwood rarely displayed tool-marks and, when present, these were usually aligned obliquely across the ends of the stems; tool-marks were more frequent on the wood chips and slivers.

Results

The wood and charcoal analyses are summarised in Table 13 and discussed below. Classification follows that of *Flora Europaea* (Tutin, Heywood *et al* 1964-80). Group names are given when anatomical differences between related genera are too slight to allow secure identification to genus level. These include members of the Pomoideae (*Crataegus, Malus, Pyrus* and *Sorbus*) and Salicaceae (*Salix* and *Populus*). Similarly, in degraded charcoal some unrelated taxa can be problematical (eg *Corylus* and *Alnus*). Where a genus is represented by a single species in the British flora this is named as the most likely origin of the wood, given the provenance and period, but it should be noted that it is rarely possible to name individual species from wood features, and exotic species of trees and shrubs were introduced to Britain from an early period (Godwin 1956; Mitchell 1974).

The anatomical structure of the charcoal was consistent with the following taxa or groups of taxa:

Betulaceae. *Alnus glutinosa* (L.) Gaertner, European alder
Caprifoliaceae. *Sambucus nigra* L, elder
Corylaceae. *Corylus avellana* L., hazel
Fagaceae. *Quercus* sp., oak
Oleaceae. *Fraxinus excelsior* L., ash
Rosaceae. Subfamilies:
Pomoideae which includes *Crataegus* spp., hawthorn; *Malus* sp., apple; *Pyrus* sp., pear; *Sorbus* spp., rowan, service tree and whitebeam. These taxa are anatomically similar; one or more taxa may be represented in the charcoal.
Rosoideae which includes *Rosa* sp., briar, and *Rubus* sp., bramble and raspberry.

Salicaceae. *Salix* spp., willow, and *Populus* spp., poplar. In most respects these taxa are anatomically similar. The ray type sometimes allows the taxon to be named; however, this feature is not always a reliable indicator, particularly for juvenile wood, and has not been used in this instance.

PHASES 2 AND 3

Three samples of waterlogged wood were examined from the fills of ditches 191 (fills 112 and 128) and 188 (fill 187), and one from a fill (129) of pit 157. Although ditch 191 was interpreted as containing cess the woody components of the three features were comparable. Each contained a mix of narrow roundwood and twiggy material (much of which was impossible to examine in detail owing to concretions of mineralised sediments), and slivers and chips from large wood, some of which included toolmarks or were partially charred; loose bark from (unidentified) large wood was also present. The samples included roundwood from hazel (*Corylus avellana*) (and also some that could only be identified as hazel or alder (*Alnus glutinosa*), ash (*Fraxinus excelsior*), the hawthorn/*Sorbus* group (Pomoideae), oak (*Quercus* sp.), bramble/raspberry (*Rubus* sp.) or briar (*Rosa* sp.), willow (*Salix* sp.) or poplar (*Populus* sp.) and elder (*Sambucus* sp.) (Table 10). Oak (*Quercus* sp.) and willow (*Salix* sp.) wood chips were also present.

Roundwood diameters (Ø) were recorded as follows:

Ditch fill 112 – elder, 1 x Ø 5mm
hazel, 1 x Ø 5mm, 2 x Ø 15mm (3 growth rings, GR)
hazel/ alder, 1 x Ø 10mm
hawthorn group, 1 x Ø 7mm (with oblique tool-mark)
oak, 1 x Ø 7mm

Ditch fill 128 - hazel, 1 x Ø 7mm, 1 x Ø 12mm
hazel/ alder, 1 x Ø 7mm
oak, 1 x Ø 6 mm, 1 x Ø 7mm, 1 x Ø 20mm (oblique tool-mark and charred)
willow/ poplar, 1 x Ø 2mm, 1 x Ø 3mm

Ditch fill 187 – alder/ hazel, 2 x Ø 10mm
briar/ bramble, 1 x Ø 5mm
willow/ poplar, 1 x Ø 5mm

Pit fill 129 - ash, 2 x Ø 12mm
hazel, 1 x Ø 3mm (3AR), 4 x Ø 10mm (5 GR), 8 x Ø 20mm (4 x 5GR, 1 x 10GR)
hawthorn group, 2 x Ø 3mm (2GR)

Although the wood structure of some of the hazel roundwood in 129 was characteristic of coppiced stems (eg wide early growth rings), some fragments were much slower grown, suggesting either a non-coppiced origin or coppice growing under stressed conditions.

PHASE 5

Wood fragments were examined from the fills of pits 139 (105), 144 (131) and 146 (107 and 127), ditch or pallisade trench 143 (133) and gully 190 (156).

In 133, the fill of pit 144, wood fragments (oak, *Quercus*) and roundwood were also abundant but often too degraded or mineralised to examine. Roundwood, identified as

hazel (*Corylus avellana*) and/or alder (*Alnus glutinosa*) and willow (*Salix* sp.) or poplar (*Populus* sp.), provided the following data:

alder/hazel, 2 x Ø 10mm, 1 x 12mm (6 GR), probably coppice stem
willow/poplar, 1 x Ø 5mm (3 GR), 1 x Ø 10mm (8 GR), 1 x Ø 15mm (11 GR).

Twiggy material and narrow roundwood up to 7mm in diameter was particularly conspicuous in the fill of gully 190 (156), but was mostly too degraded to identify to species. Measurements from alder (*Alnus glutinosa*) and the hawthorn/*Sorbus* group (Pomoideae) were recorded as follows:

alder, 1 x Ø 3mm, 1 x Ø 5mm, 1 x Ø 7mm
hawthorn group, 1 x Ø 3mm

A number of abraded and surface worn fragments from large wood, including some probable wood-working chips, were identified as alder (*Alnus glutinosa*), the hawthorn/*Sorbus* group (Pomoideae) and oak (*Quercus* sp.).

Deposit 211 was of particular interest because hammerscale and slag occurred in the same context. Since evidence of iron-working was only slight it was thought that the process was not conducted within the area of excavation. Other deposits from the feature included domestic debris (the remains of various types of food-stuff) and a large volume of charcoal. The latter was almost exclusively made up of pieces of oak (*Quercus* sp.) heartwood from mature wood (ie wide roundwood, cordwood or trunkwood); fragments measured up to about 10^3mm. Other taxa identified included hazel (*Corylus avellana*) and alder (*Alnus glutinosa*) (see Table 10).

The wooden constituents from the fill of ditch 143 also differed somewhat to those from the other contexts examined. The sample consisted entirely of small wood chips/slivers (some charred) and there was scant evidence of narrow roundwood. Material examined included oak (*Quercus* sp.) heartwood and loose bark from large wood. Food debris and hammerscale were also recorded from the feature. It seems likely that the wood represents firewood, although structural remains cannot be ruled out.

The fill (105) of pit 139 included four pieces of split roundwood, roughly 25mm in radius, and with at least 33 narrow growth rings. These were identified as from a member of the hawthorn/*Sorbus* group (Pomoideae) and probably originated from a single piece of roundwood. Narrow Pomoideae roundwood (diameter 10mm, 10 GR) was also present, together with a sliver of alder (*Alnus glutinosa*) wood.

The fill (127) of pit 146 included narrow roundwood from willow (*Salix* sp.) or poplar (*Populus* sp.), the hawthorn/*Sorbus* group (Pomoideae) and probably ash (*Fraxinus excelsior*) which provided the follows measurements:

?ash, 1 x Ø 2mm (2 GR)
hawthorn group, 1 x Ø 3mm (4 GR), 1 x Ø 10mm (4 GR)
willow/poplar, 1 x Ø 7mm, 3 x Ø 10mm (2 x 5 GR, 1 x 7 GR).

Wood chips and fragments from large wood from oak (*Quercus* sp.) and a piece of carbonised alder (*Alnus glutinosa*) roundwood approximately 70mm in diameter were also included in sample 10, together with a large quantity of loose bark flakes from unidentified wide roundwood or trunkwood. In addition there were numerous twiggy pieces (many <0.5mm in diameter) that were too degraded to identify from structural features; morphologically, however, they were comparable to heather (*Erica* or *Calluna*).

PHASE 6

Faecal waste was also frequent in 160, the fill of slot 140. In common with the organic material from cesspit 144 and ditch 191, the wood remains were mostly too mineralised or degraded to identify. Fragments examined included roundwood from alder (*Alnus glutinosa*) and willow (*Salix* sp.) or poplar (*Populus* sp.) which probably derived from coppice rods. Oblique tool-marks where stems had been cut or chopped were evident on some pieces. The following data was recorded:

alder, 1 x Ø 5mm (3 GR), 1 x Ø 10mm
willow/poplar, 1 x Ø 10mm (9 GR), 2 x Ø 12mm (9 GR)
– matching growth
patterns in these fragments suggested an origin from the same stem.

Fragments of worked oak (*Quercus* sp.) wood were also present, and, in addition, part of a partially hollowed out artefact made from oak roundwood (diameter roughly 25mm). The function of the artefact was not clear. It is possible that the willow and alder roundwood also derived from artefactual use, eg wattlework, although it was not possible to substantiate this suggestion.

Discussion

The pits and ditches which were studied contained large quantities of wood, which had been preserved through waterlogging. Charcoal was also common but not as abundant as the wood. Wood samples were examined from Phases 2, 3, 5 and 6, and proved to be similar in content and character throughout these phases (Table 13).

Wood samples consisted of roundwood and twiggy fragments up to about 20mm in diameter (usually with the bark *in situ*), and wood chips and slivers from large wood. Tool-marks on the roundwood were rare but demonstrated where stems had been cut or chopped, eg hawthorn (112) and oak (128); the latter was also partially charred. In addition, some stems, eg the alder/hazel in pit 144, included wide early rings characteristic of coppice growth. The use of roundwood for artefactual purposes was demonstrated by a fragment from a carved item of unknown function, recovered from a possible latrine context (fill of slot 140) - in this instance using oak.

Cess deposits in pit 144, ditch 191 and slot 140 inferred the use of these features as possible latrines. The presence of other waste materials in these contexts, eg animal bones, wood, roundwood and twigs, and other plant remains, however suggested a more general use for the disposal of rubbish.

A possible origin for the wood therefore seems to be fourfold:

i) the remains of narrow roundwood (up to 20mm in diameter) and sometimes slivers from large wood, either from artefactual use, eg wattlework, or from domestic fuel debris dumped with other household waste, eg from food preparation;

ii) the disposal of stems and branches from the clearance of undergrowth or hedgerows;

iii) the natural accumulation of debris from fallen twigs and stems from surrounding vegetation;

iv) deposited debris from wood-working waste (wood chips), some of which may have been used as fuel or disposed of by burning.

Roundwood bearing tool-marks, charred portions or attributed as coppice wood clearly derived as an end-product from specific activities, eg fuel, wattlework or other artefactual uses, clearance of undergrowth, hedge-prunnings, etc. The low incidence of charring on the roundwood suggests that some ratio of the wood derived from uses other than as fuel.

Roundwood included both coppiced and non-coppiced stems – the latter from narrow stems/branches and twigs. While a high proportion of the roundwood was too degraded or mineralised to identify using anatomical methods (see above), the morphology allowed some to be provisionally named as either hawthorn and/or blackthorn (*Prunus spinosa*), and heather (the latter in pit 146). Twigs and roundwood from the hawthorn/*Sorbus* group were identified (anatomically) from all samples except those from Phase 7, but neither blackthorn nor heather were recorded. It seems likely that the narrower roundwood and fine twigs probably accumulated naturally in these open features either from fallen tree debris or, given the proximity to the Pool, detritus washed in with flood water.

Wood chips from tree felling, conversion of timber or carpentry waste verified the use of timber from oak (*Quercus* sp.), ash (*Fraxinus excelsior*), alder (*Alnus glutinosa*), the hawthorn/*Sorbus* group (Pomoideae), willow (*Salix* sp.) or poplar (*Populus* sp.) and possibly hazel (*Corylus avellana*). It was not possible to assess the dimensions of the timbers used apart from noting that all the chips related to large wood (ie wide roundwood, trunkwood or cordwood). Most samples also included scales of bark from large wood and, although leather was found in pit 157 and ditch 191, there was no evidence to suggest on-site tanning, and it is more likely that the bark and wood chips originated from a common source.

Domestic and industrial fuels
In view of the quantities of domestic waste (eg meat bones and seashells) in the contexts examined it seems likely that at least some of the wood remains would represent debris from domestic firewood, even though relatively few fragments showed evidence of burning. Thus firewood consisted of a mixture of roundwood, with at least some from coppiced sources, and oddments of wood, eg woodworking waste, as and when available.

In contrast, the large charcoal deposit in context 211 consisted almost entirely of small pieces of oak (*Quercus* sp.) heartwood from either roundwood, cordwood or trunkwood of fairly wide dimension. The percentage of hazel (*Corylus avellana*) and alder (*Alnus glutinosa*) present was negligible. This deposit clearly differed in origin from those described above and demonstrated a preference for mature oak. The feature also contained hammerscale and slag from iron-smithing and, by association, the charcoal may have represented spent industrial fuel, which would almost certainly have been used as prepared charcoal.

Environmental evidence
Evidence of the deliberate raising of the ground levels in Phase 1 and the rich deposits of aquatic organisms in the soils and sediments suggested that rising ground water was a frequent problem. Wetland species, including alder (*Alnus glutinosa*) and willow (*Salix* sp.), would almost certainly have been prevalent in this environment, and wood remains in the pits attested to the economic use of both taxa.

Ash (*Fraxinus excelsior*), oak (*Quercus* sp.) and hazel (*Corylus avellana*) also tolerate a certain amount of dampness (although not waterlogging), but generally prefer dryer soils. Twig morphology identified either or both hawthorn (*Crateagus* sp.) and blackthorn (*Prunus spinosa*), and also heather (*Erica* sp./*Calluna* sp.), although only the hawthorn/*Sorbus* group (Pomoideae) was recorded from the wood structure. Heather is indicative of heathland, poor soils and sometimes wetland. Elder (*Sambucus* sp.) was also recorded from the site; elders commonly grow on nitrogen-rich soils around habitation or in marginal woodland/scrub.

Fast-grown stems characteristic of coppice growth were recorded from hazel, alder and willow/poplar from Phases 3, 6 and 7 (see Table 13), although some stems included much slower growth, which could suggest either a non-coppiced origin or coppice growing in stressed conditions. Coppice stems of both oak and ash regenerate

Table 13: Charcoal and waterlogged wood from Phases 2, 3, 5 and 6

Phase	Context	Feature type	Alder *Alnus*	Hazel *Corylus*	Ash *Fraxinus*	Pear *Pomoideae*	Oak *Quercus*	Rose/cherry *Rosa/Rubus*	Willow *Salicaceae*	Elder *Sambucus*	Loose bark
Phase 2											
	187	Fill of ditch 188, w/w	(2r)	(2r)	2 s/c	-	21h s/c, 3r	1r	1r	-	7
Phase 3											
	112	Fill of ditch 191, w/w	-	4r	-	1r	3h s/c, 1r	-	-	1r	1
	128		(1s/c)	(1s/c) 2r	-	1r	5h s/c, 3r	-	1 s/c, 2r	-	6
	129	Fill of pit 157, w/w	-	13r	2r	2r	2s/c	-	-	-	6
Phase 5A											
	156	Fill of slot 190, w/w	5s/c, 3r	-	-	2s/c, 1r	11h s/c, 2s	-	-	-	12
Phase 5B											
	131	Fill of pit 144, w/w	(3r)	(3r)	-	-	3h	-	3r	-	-
	105	Fill of pit 139, w/w	1s/c	-	-	5r	-	-	-	-	-
	127	Fill of pit 146,w/w	1s/ c,1r	-	1r	4r	3h	-	8r	-	43
Phase 6											
	133	Fill of ditch 143, w/w	-	-	-	-	13h s/c	-	-	-	7
	160	Fill of slot 140, w/w	2r	-	-	-	1s s/c, 1h	-	3r	-	-
		Wooden artefact, w/w	-	-	-	-	1r	-	-	-	-
Phase 7											
	211	In layer 210	1	1	-	-	298h	-	-	-	-

Key. h =heartwood; s = sapwood; r = roundwood (diameter <20mm); s/c = sliver/ chip; w/w = waterlogged wood
When *Alnus* can not be distinguished from *Corylus*, the entry is given in brackets for both
The number of fragments identified is indicated

more slowly than, for example, hazel and willow (Morgan 1982) and it was therefore more difficult to determine whether the oak and ash roundwood was obtained from a coppiced source. Manorial records from the 11th century show that managed woodlands were well established throughout England by this time and were often under considerable pressure to provide sufficient resources for local communities (Rackham 1976).

Fruit stones from sloe (blackthorn), cherry, plum and probably bullace were present in several contexts, as were raspberry or blackberry pips. While sloe, blackberry and possibly cherry would have been available from trees or shrubs growing in the countryside, plum and bullace testify to the cultivation of *Prunus*. Prunnings from cultivated fruit trees (possibly also including apples, pears etc) would have provided a useful and alternative source of wood, timber and kindling. The woody stems from either blackberry, raspberry or briar (Rosoideae) were recorded in the fill of ditch 188.

Conclusion

This report includes the identification of deposits of waterlogged wood and charcoal from features (mainly pits) associated with an 11th/12th-century settlement on the edge of Brayford Pool. Taxa identified included oak (*Quercus* sp.), ash (*Fraxinus excelsior*), hazel (*Corylus avellana*), alder (*Alnus glutinosa*), the hawthorn/*Sorbus* group (Pomoideae), willow (*Salix* sp.) or poplar (*Populus* sp.), elder (*Sambucus* sp.) and bramble/raspberry (*Rubus* sp.) or briar (*Rosa* sp.). The wood deposits mostly consisted of narrow roundwood probably from both coppiced and non-coppiced sources but also included twiggy material (probably fallen twigs etc from local vegetation) and wood chips and slivers from large wood (mostly attributed as wood-working waste). Tool-marks and charring indicated that a fair proportion derived from artefactual uses, eg wattlework or chopped firewood, or possibly from clearing undergrowth or hedges. Some of the wood probably represented domestic fuel and this contrasted with evidence of (probable) industrial fuel debris (charcoal) which consisted almost exclusively of mature oak.

Environmental evidence indicated the ready availability of wetland species, eg alder and willow, which would have been consistent with the damp/wet soils of the area. The remaining taxa identified were indicative of dryer soils, possibly with some heathland. Managed woodland including alder, willow/poplar and hazel was also present.

Parasite eggs
by John Carrott

Introduction

Seven small subsamples were submitted to Palaeoecology Research Services (PRS) by the Environmental Archaeology Consultancy (EAC) for an investigation of their content of the eggs of intestinal parasitic nematodes. Four of the subsamples were thought to be of faecal waste and the others were submitted as controls in order to determine if parasite eggs occurred more generally in the deposits.

Methods

The samples were examined for the eggs of intestinal parasitic nematodes using the 'squash' technique of Dainton (1992). Measurements of maximum length (including and excluding polar plugs) and maximum width were taken using a calibrated eyepiece graticule at 600x magnification and subsequently converted to microns.

Although primarily for the detection of intestinal parasitic nematode eggs the 'squash' technique routinely reveals other microfossil remains; where present (or markedly absent) these have also been noted.

The size range quoted for *Trichuris trichiura* (Linnaeus) follows that given by Ash and Orihel (1984). Significantly larger *T. trichiura* eggs are occasionally reported in modern parasitological samples—this is usually in response to the use of anthelmintics, or may be a confusion with *T. vulpis* which children sometimes acquire through geophagia. Size ranges for the eggs of trichurids of other common domestic animals are from several sources including Kassai (1998) and the WWW pages of the College of Veterinary Medicine, University of Missouri-Columbia.

Results

The results of the initial investigations to determine the presence/absence and state of preservation of parasite eggs are presented below in context number order. Where eggs were present a brief summary of the additional work undertaken is also given.

Context 105 (fill of pit 139)
The 'squash' was mostly organic detritus with a little inorganic material. Many fragments of phytolith and a few fungal hyphae and pollen grains were noted but no parasite eggs were seen.

Context 112 (fill of ditch 191)
Mostly organic detritus with some inorganic material and a few pollen grains. Ten trichurid eggs and a single ?*Ascaris* were also noted. A further six slides were prepared in order for measurements of the eggs to be made. Approximately half of the eggs seen were sufficiently well preserved to be measurable and a total of 32 measurements of trichurid eggs and three of unfertilised ascarid eggs were taken. Fourteen of the *Trichuris* eggs measured retained both of their polar plugs, five had one polar plug, and the remainder none.

Context 128 (fill of ditch 191)
Mostly organic detritus with some inorganic material and a few diatoms. Four *Trichuris* eggs were also seen in the initial 'squash' and fourteen further slides were prepared. The preservation of the eggs in this sample was extremely variable and many were too poorly preserved to be measurable. A total of 18 trichurid eggs (only five of which had retained both polar plugs with a further four having one) and two unfertilised *Ascaris* were measured.

Context 129 (fill of pit 157)
The 'squash' was mostly organic detritus with a little inorganic material and some phytolith fragments, diatoms, fungal spores, and pollen grains. No parasite eggs were seen.

Context 131 (fill of pit 144)
Approximately half organic detritus and half inorganic material with many diatoms (of several forms), and a few live 'soil' ?nematodes and fungal hyphae. Seven *Trichuris* eggs were seen in the initial 'squash' and a further three slides were prepared for measurements to be taken. Six measurements of *Ascaris* eggs (all unfertilised) were taken and 33 of *Trichuris* eggs (thirteen with both polar plugs, three with one plug, and 17 with none). Three of the trichurid eggs were particularly well preserved.

Context 153 (fill of pit 152)
The 'squash' was mostly of organic detritus with some inorganic material and a few diatoms. No parasite eggs were seen.

Context 160 (fill of slot 140)
The initial 'squash' was mostly organic detritus with a little inorganic material and some fungal hyphae. Six *Trichuris* and two *Ascaris* eggs were seen and a further

three slides prepared for measurements to be made. Thirty-one *Trichuris* and four unfertilised *Ascaris* eggs were measured; eleven of the *Trichuris* eggs had both polar plugs, eight had one, and the remainder none. Three of the trichurid eggs were particularly well preserved.

Discussion

Identification of trichurids to species from their eggs is problematic in that the size ranges for different species often overlap significantly (Fig 16). In the case of the remains from this site the problem is to distinguish between *Trichuris trichiura*, the whipworm of humans, and *T. suis* (Schrank), of pigs; a particularly difficult task given that the usual size range for *T. trichiura* is a wholly contained subset of that for *T. suis*. Table 14 shows the egg measurements for each sample and Figure 16 shows the measurements with commonly quoted size ranges for *T. trichiura* and other trichurids of some common domesticated animals given as boxed overlays. Figure

Table 14: Measurements for trichurid eggs in microns

Context 112			Context 131			Context 128			Context 160		
p-p	xpp	w	p-p	xpp	w	p-p	xpp	w	p-p	xpp	w
*52.12	46.29	25.71	56.57	46.29	23.14	*54.26	48.86	23.79	*51.66	45.00	25.71
48.86	43.71	23.79	52.07	47.57	23.14	*52.97	47.57	24.43	*50.37	43.71	24.43
52.71	43.71	25.71	*56.31	49.50	24.43	*50.40	45.00	23.14	54.00	46.29	23.14
*57.27	51.43	22.50	*53.74	46.93	24.43	*54.26	48.86	25.71	*54.23	47.57	23.14
51.43	47.57	22.50	52.71	47.57	25.71	*52.97	47.57	23.14	*53.59	46.93	24.43
*52.12	46.29	26.36	*54.39	47.57	22.50	51.43	46.29	24.43	*54.87	48.21	23.79
*55.34	49.50	25.71	*55.67	48.86	23.14	52.71	45.00	23.79	48.86	43.07	25.07
*52.12	46.29	23.14	*53.10	46.29	25.07	*50.40	45.00	23.79	48.86	45.00	23.14
56.57	46.29	23.14	*53.10	46.29	25.07	*52.33	46.93	23.79	*54.23	47.57	22.50
57.86	54.00	23.14	*56.96	50.14	23.79	*50.40	45.00	21.86	*52.95	46.29	23.14
*54.69	48.86	23.14	55.29	46.29	23.14	48.86	46.29	22.50	*53.59	46.93	23.79
*54.69	48.86	23.79	*53.10	46.29	25.71	*51.69	46.29	21.21	*50.37	43.71	25.71
*52.12	46.29	25.71	*54.39	47.57	23.79	54.00	48.86	23.14	52.71	46.93	25.07
54.00	46.93	24.43	51.43	46.93	23.14	*52.33	46.93	23.14	*54.23	47.57	24.43
*52.77	46.93	25.07	*57.60	50.79	24.43	*52.97	47.57	22.50	*52.95	46.29	23.14
50.79	46.93	25.07	55.93	45.64	23.14	55.29	48.86	23.14	*52.95	46.29	22.50
*46.98	41.14	24.43	*55.67	48.86	23.14	*51.69	46.29	23.14	52.07	46.93	23.14
*52.12	46.29	25.71	*54.39	47.57	24.43	*51.69	46.29	22.50	54.64	46.93	24.43
48.86	45.64	23.14	*55.67	48.86	23.14				*52.30	45.64	23.14
*52.77	46.93	23.14	*55.03	48.21	24.43				51.43	46.29	25.71
50.79	45.00	25.71	54.00	46.29	23.79				54.00	46.93	23.14
*54.05	48.21	23.79	54.64	47.57	20.57				56.57	47.57	23.14
51.43	43.71	22.50	*52.46	45.64	24.43				*57.45	50.79	24.43
52.71	48.21	25.07	56.57	46.29	24.43				55.29	48.86	23.14
53.36	48.21	24.43	*55.67	48.86	25.71				*56.16	49.50	25.07
*49.55	43.71	22.50	*53.10	46.29	22.50				57.21	47.57	23.79
*52.12	46.29	25.71	51.43	46.29	24.43				*57.45	50.79	23.79
54.64	48.21	23.79	54.00	48.86	22.50				*53.59	46.93	23.14
*57.27	51.43	25.71	*54.39	47.57	25.71				*54.23	47.57	25.71
54.64	48.86	23.14	53.36	48.86	23.14				*53.59	46.93	25.71
*52.77	46.93	24.43	*54.39	47.57	23.14				*55.52	48.86	21.86
*55.34	49.50	23.14	52.71	47.57	24.43						
			*53.10	46.29	23.14						

Key: p-p = polar plug to polar plug maximum length; xpp = maximum length excluding polar plugs; w = maximum width. Where possible, measurements were taken directly from the eggs but polar plug to polar plug measurements are calculated from the length excluding polar plugs where asterisked

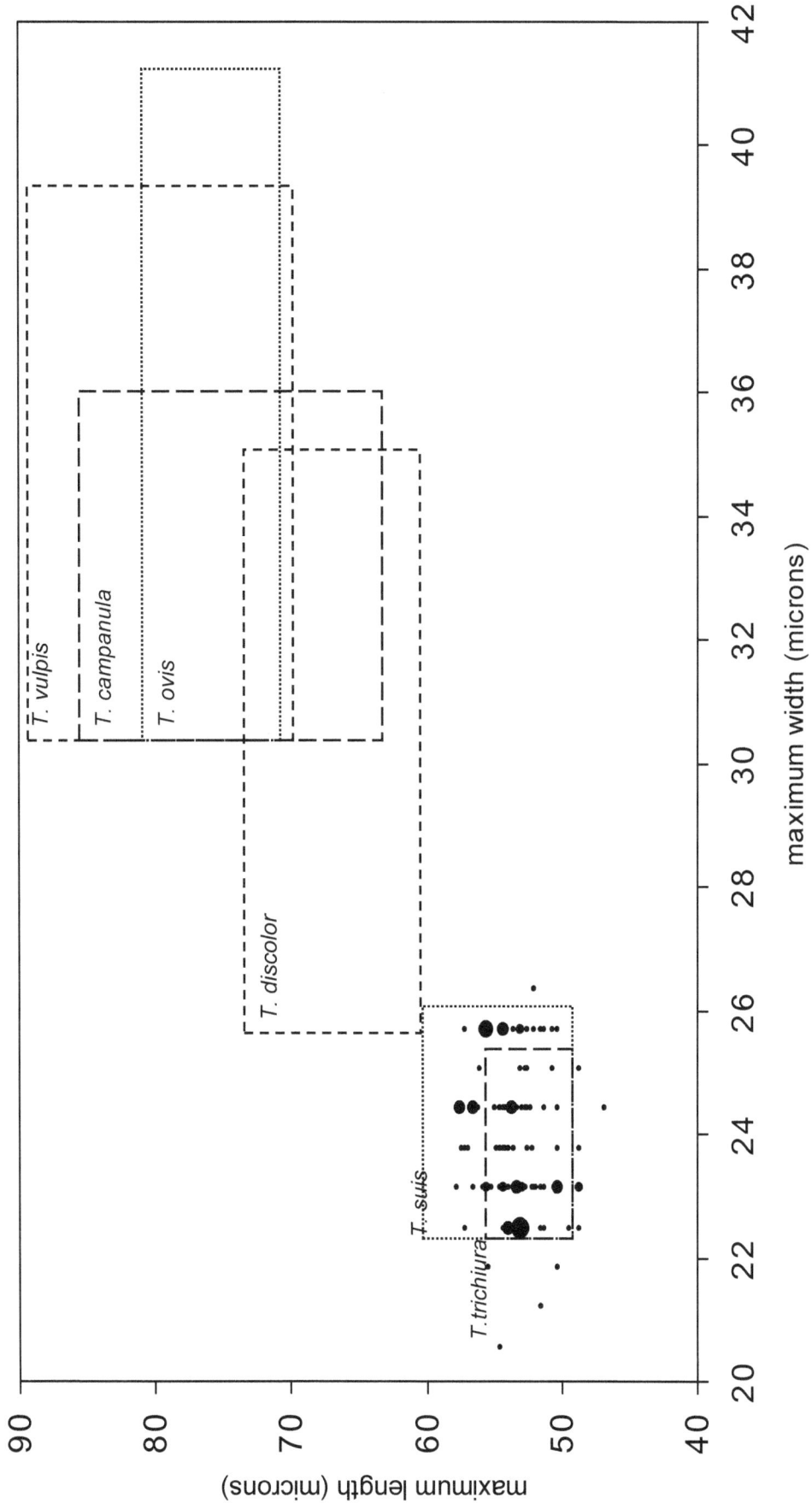

Fig 16: Plotted trichurid egg measurements with overlay of size ranges for eggs of trichurids of several common domesticated animals and *Trichuris trichiura*

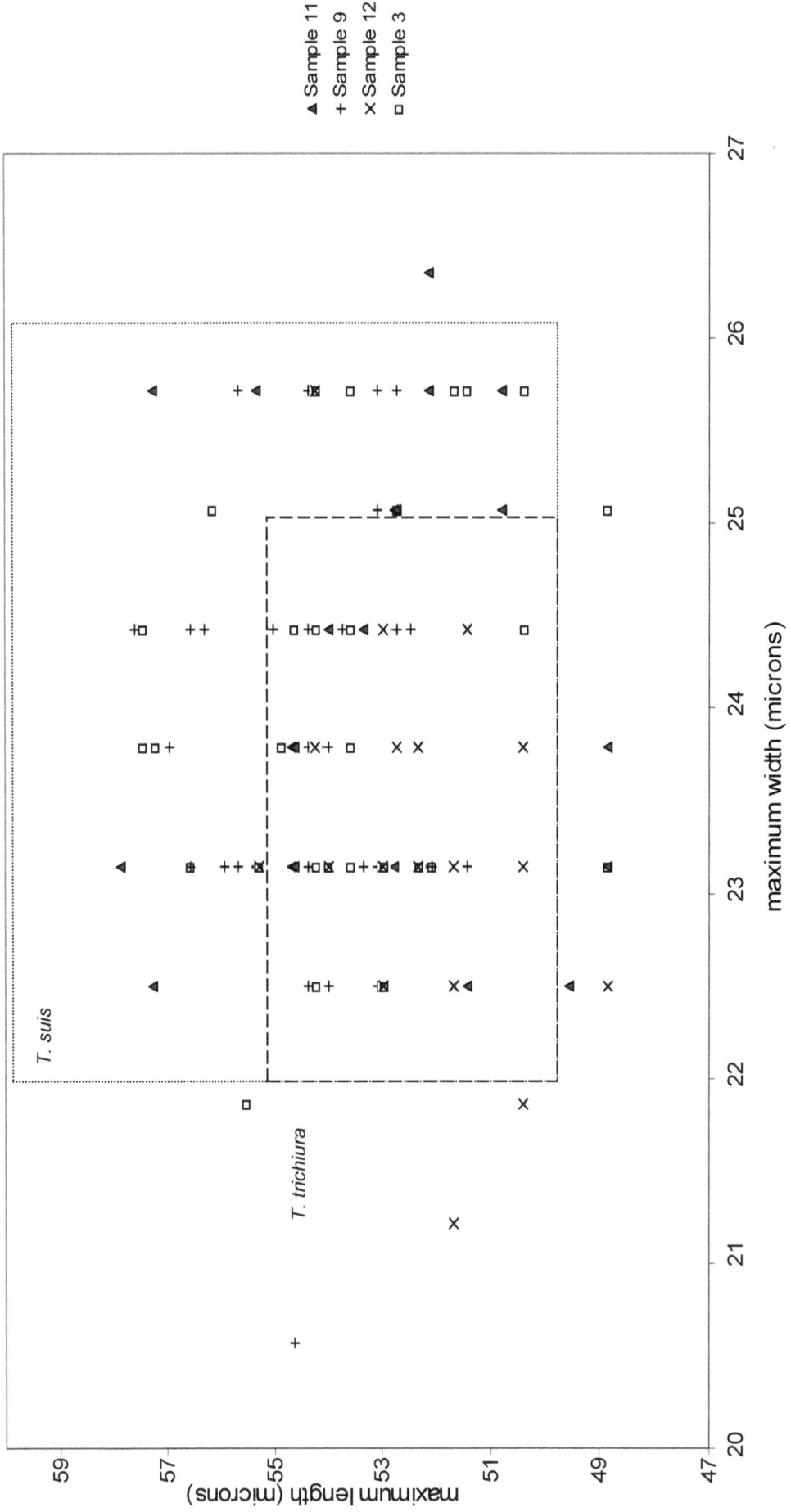

Fig 17: Plotted *Trichuris* measurements by sample

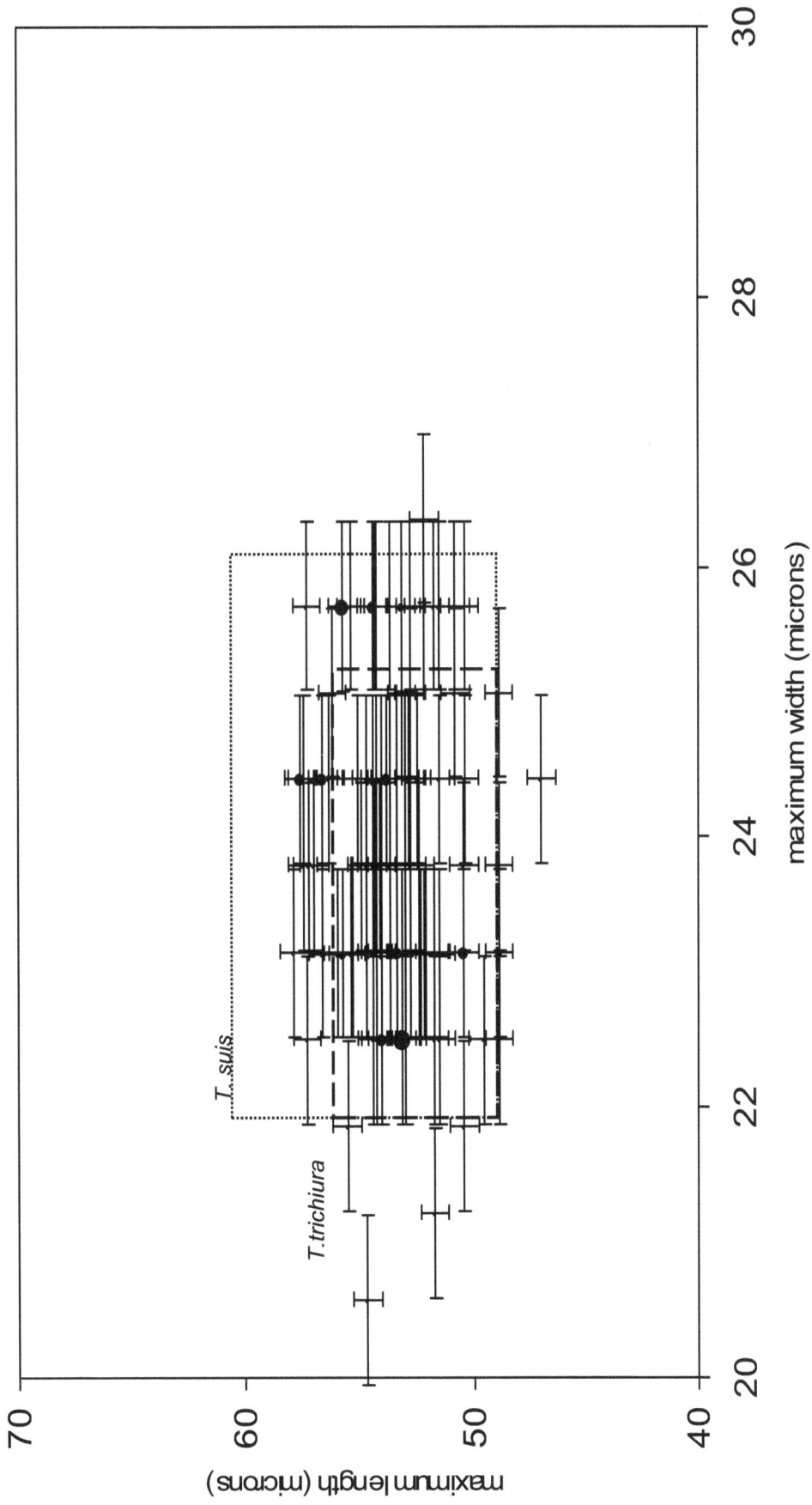

Fig 18: Plotted trichurid egg measurements with overlay of size ranges for eggs of *Trichuris trichiura* and *T. suis*

Table 15: Descriptive statistics for polar plug to polar plug maximum length (l) and maximum width (w) measurements (in microns) by sample

	Context 112 Sample 11 (l)	Context 131 Sample 9 (l)	Context 128 Sample 12 (l)	Context 160 Sample 3 (l)	Context 112 Sample 11 (w)	Context 131 Sample 9 (w)	Context 128 Sample 12 (w)	Context 160 Sample 3 (w)
Mean	52.96	54.33	52.26	53.61	24.23	23.84	23.29	23.95
Standard Error	0.45	0.28	0.39	0.40	0.22	0.20	0.24	0.20
Median	52.74	54.39	52.33	53.59	24.11	23.79	23.14	23.79
Mode	52.12	54.39	52.97	54.23	25.71	23.14	23.14	23.14
Standard Deviation	2.53	1.61	1.64	2.23	1.23	1.14	1.02	1.10
Sample Variance	6.42	2.58	2.68	4.98	1.50	1.30	1.05	1.21
Kurtosis	0.08	-0.73	-0.15	0.01	-1.45	0.74	1.13	-0.94
Skewness	-0.11	0.10	-0.14	-0.29	0.12	-0.32	0.28	0.29
Range	10.88	6.17	6.43	8.59	3.86	5.14	4.50	3.86
Minimum	46.98	51.43	48.86	48.86	22.50	20.57	21.21	21.86
Maximum	57.86	57.60	55.29	57.45	26.36	25.71	25.71	25.71
Sum	1694.85	1792.93	940.63	1661.91	775.29	786.86	419.14	742.50
Count	32.00	33.00	18.00	31.00	32.00	33.00	18.00	31.00

17 shows the measurements labelled by sample but no clear grouping by sample is evident. Figure 18 shows the measurement data on shorter scale axes including error bars.

Several of the data points fall wholly outside the ranges (allowing for error) for either *T. trichiura* or *T. suis*. These may represent aberrant eggs, or could reflect 'in-ground' changes in egg morphology (all of the overlay boxes for egg size ranges are based on limited sets of published 'modern' data). No real study of changes in egg morphology caused by varying ground conditions and states of preservation has been undertaken and comparison with modern data, though valid, must, of necessity, be cautious. However, most of the measurements fall within the range for modern *T. trichiura* and almost all within the range for *T. suis*.

Mean values for polar plug to polar plug maximum length and maximum width for each sample were calculated and are presented, along with other summary descriptive statistics for each sample, in Table 15. However, frequency plots for the data for each sample and for the combined data from all samples (Fig 19) show indications of a bimodal distribution in some cases (particularly in 112 and to a lesser extent in 160) which would be expected if two species were present. That individual data points for the measurements fall outside the size ranges given for both modern *T. trichiura* and *T. suis* is perhaps most likely to be due to taphonomic processes but objective investigation of the effects of, for example, different soil chemistries on egg morphology has yet to be undertaken.

Similarly, the eggs of the ascarids *Ascaris lumbricoides* (Linnaeus) and *A. suum* (Goeze), the maw worms of humans and pigs respectively (though some parasitologists believe that there is just one species of *Ascaris* that infests both humans and pigs) are almost identical. The measurements obtained for the unfertilised *Ascaris* eggs seen in these samples (Table 16) could indicate the presence of either human or pig faeces, or both. Taylor (1955) has remarked that a low ratio of

Table 16: Measurements of unfertilised Ascaris eggs from all samples (in microns)

Context 131	66.86	by	48.86
	72.00	by	56.57
	72.00	by	51.43
	68.14	by	47.57
	79.71	by	56.57
	66.86	by	51.43
Context 160	65.57	by	55.29
	66.86	by	56.57
Context 112	64.29	by	57.86
	73.28	by	51.43
	72.00	by	64.29
	69.43	by	54.00
	77.14	by	51.43
Context 128	69.43	by	54.00
	69.43	by	61.71

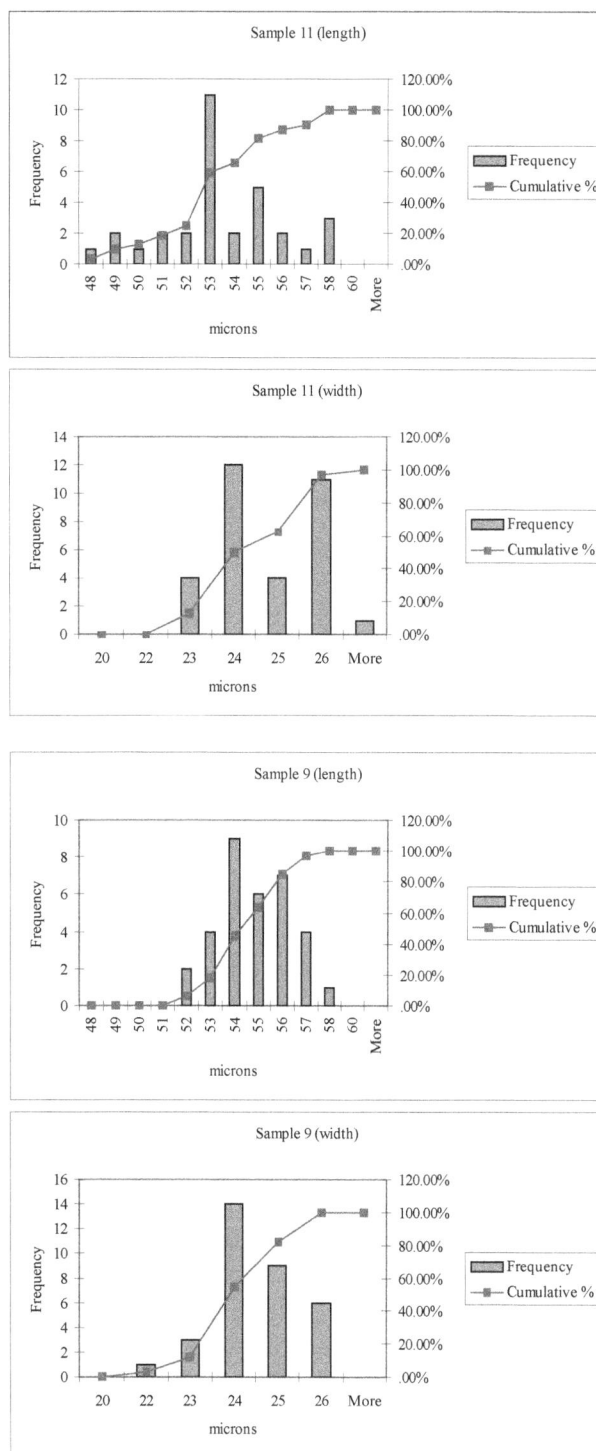

Fig 19a: Histograms of the distributions of polar plug to polar plug, maximum length and maximum width measurements (samples 9 and 11)

Ascaris to *Trichuris* eggs, as is the case with all of the samples considered here, may indicate human rather than pig faeces.

In summary, all of the samples from deposits interpreted as 'cess' did indeed contain faecal material, as indicated by the presence of the eggs of intestinal parasitic nematodes, whereas none of the 'control' samples gave any eggs. It has not been possible to determine definitively the source

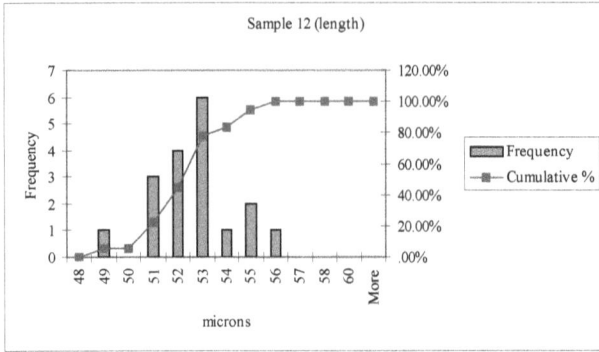

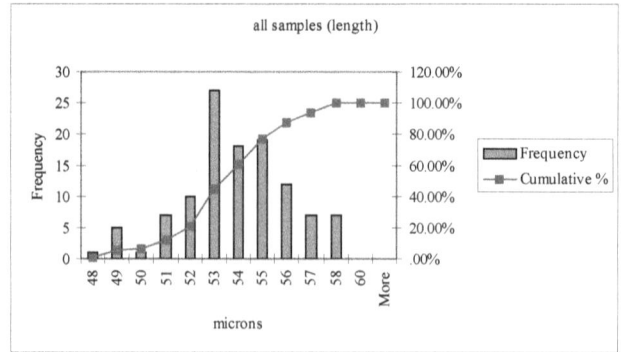

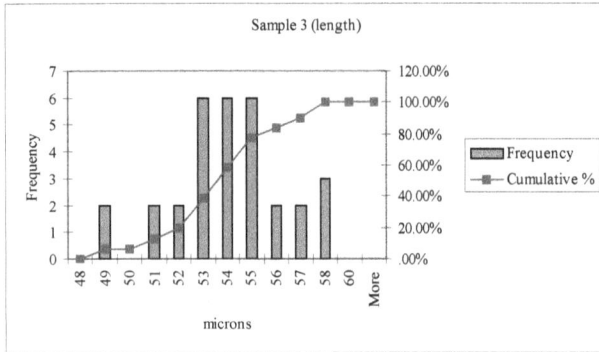

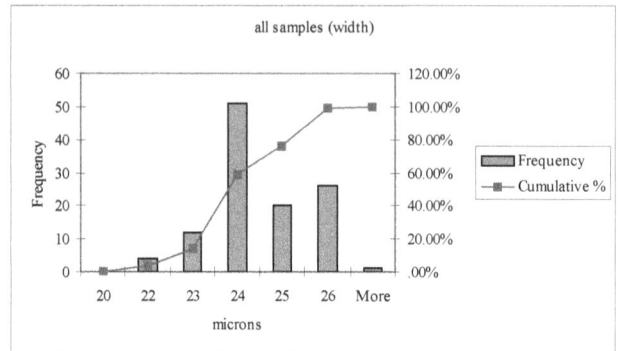

Fig 19b: Histograms of the distributions of polar plug to polar plug, maximum length (samples 12 and 3)

Fig 19c: Histograms of the distributions of polar plug to polar plug, maximum width (samples 12 and 3)

Fig 19d: Histograms of the distributions of polar plug to polar plug, maximum length and width (all samples)

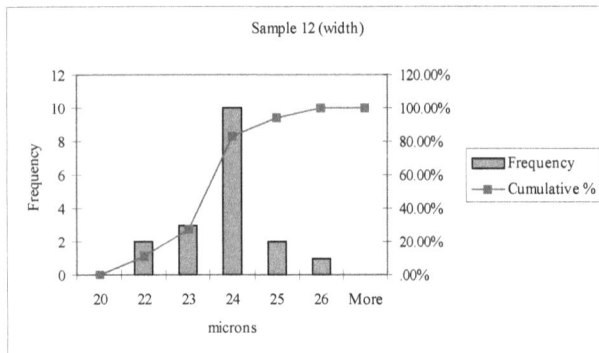

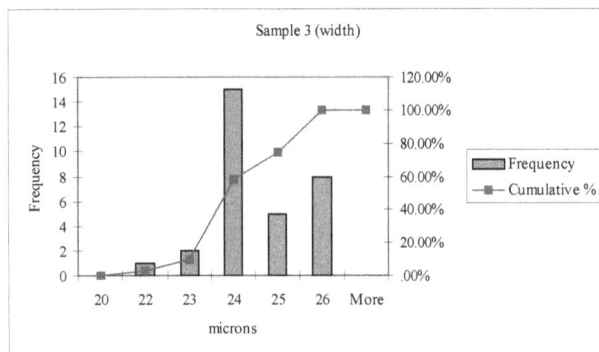

from 160 or 153), showing their presence at the site, and some of the straw/hay recorded from several of the contexts may have been from cleared bedding for these animals.

Fish bones
by Alison Locker

The following species were identified from these late 11th to early 12th-century deposits; eel (*Anguilla anguilla*), herring (*Clupea harengus*), pike (*Esox lucius*), roach (*Rutilius rutilus*), cod *(Gadus morhua)*, Gadidae and perch (*Perca fluviatilis*). These are tabulated below in order of phase.

See Table 1 for details of the deposits.

In the 'indet' category only potentially identifiable bones are included, in this instance they are vertebrae.

The species identified show both fresh water and marine exploitation. Eel, pike, roach and perch, all of which would have been eaten, would have been readily available from the Pool and local rivers, and at a distance of only 35 miles from the coast the most common marine food fishes, herring, cod and other gadids, were also available. This small sample includes those species already identified from ZEA and ZEB 95 and adds perch to the freshwater list, also identified by Irving (1996) from Lincoln.

None of the bones were from fish remarkable for their size. Cod were represented by vertebrae, both precaudal and caudal, and a large gadid fragment of ceratohyal

of the faecal content but, on balance, it seems most likely that the deposits contain both human and pig faeces. Pig bone was recorded from most of the deposits (but not

Table 17: Fish bones recovered from the soil samples

Context	112	185	129	106	127	107	131	105	133	211	210	Total
Phase	3	2	3	4	5B	5B	5B	5B	6	7	7	
Sample	11	13	6	4	10	15	9	1	18	8	19	
Eel	0	0	0	1	0	0	0	0	0	2	0	3
Herring	0	1	0	1	0	0	0	0	1	2	0	5
Pike	1	0	1	1	0	0	0	0	0	1	0	4
Roach	0	0	0	1	0	0	0	0	0	0	0	1
Cod	1	0	1	0	1	0	0	1	0	0	0	4
Sm Gadid	0	0	0	1	0	0	0	0	0	0	0	1
L Gadid	2	0	0	0	1	1	0	0	1	1	0	6
Perch	0	0	1	0	0	0	1	0	0	0	0	2
Indet	0	0	0	0	0	0	0	0	0	3	1	4
Total	4	1	3	5	2	1	1	1	2	9	1	30

See Table 1 for details of the deposits
In the 'indet' category only potentially identifiable bones are included, in this instance they are vertebrae.

showed a possible cut mark. A pike preopercular from 129 was from a fish around 56 cms in total length and a perch preopercular from a fish around 25 cms in total length. Two fish bones were among the hand collected bone assemblage and have been identified as a cod dentary and a large gadid vertebra. Both these bones indicated much larger fishes than those recovered from the soil samples.

There was no evidence from the condition of the bones in pits of cess material, although an unidentified small vertebra from layer 211 was encrusted and showed evidence of compression.

Animal bones
by Karen Deighton

A total of 7.71kg of animal bone was recovered from the site, largely deriving from 11th to 12th-century deposits. This excludes the small quantity from the bulk samples. Identifications were made with the aid of Schmidt (1972) and Cohen and Serjeantson (1996). For each element the following were recorded, where possible: taxon, fusion, side, modification, butchery and fragmentation. Recording follows Halstead (1985) and uses MinA.U. (minimum anatomical unit). The presence of ribs and vertebra was noted but they were not included in the quantification. Evidence for butchery follows Binford (1981). Assessment of ovicaprid tooth wear is after Payne (1973) and cattle tooth wear follows Halstead (1985) after Payne (1973).

The animal bone was reasonably well preserved, with a high incidence of fragmentation (58.3% of bones exhibiting breaks). This could have been due to trampling, crushing or possibly butchery. There was little surface abrasion and the majority of the bones had been stained black, probably due to a combination of chemical reaction with the organic silt matrix and water-logging. Evidence for canid gnawing was only observed on 12 elements, which would, to some extent, rule out the effects of differential preservation (Payne 1985). Some of the bone, predominantly from context 127, had been burnt. There was a low incidence of neonates, evidence confined to a single cow metapodial.

The assemblage was dominated by cattle, closely followed by ovicaprid, with a smaller percentage of pig.

Any discussion of carcass utilisation is tentative, due to the thin distribution of body parts for each of the major species. However, for cattle the lack of cranial elements could suggest these were arriving on site as dressed carcasses. An apparent domination of tibia was noted, which is surprising as the proximal tibia is usually poorly preserved (Brain 1981). This could suggest that individual joints of meat were being brought to site. For ovicaprids distribution seems fairly even, with absences corresponding to poorly preserved elements such as the distal humerus. For pig, numbers were too small for any observations to be meaningful, although it can be noted that a few more pig bones were identified in the sieved samples (Rackham, below)

Only 17 instances of butchery were noted (4.4% of identified bone); this appeared to be largely indicative of chopping, suggesting butchery was heavy-handed and concerned with jointing and dismembering.

The number of mandibles was too small to establish a coherent kill-off pattern; however, for ovicaprids the majority appears to be between 8 and 10 years old. The low numbers of neonates could suggest husbandry was not taking place on the site.

Broad comparisons with contemporary urban sites in York (Bond and O'Connor 1999), suggest a similar dominance of cattle with slightly fewer ovicaprids and a much smaller numbers of pigs. However, comparisons with assemblages from Northampton (Robinson and Wilson 1983) show a dominance of sheep, with the same smaller numbers of pigs.

The assemblage appears to represent domestic waste and is fairly typical (in broad terms) of a small medieval urban assemblage.

Table 18: Animal species present by anatomical element

Element	Cow (Bos)	Sheep/goat (Ovicaprid)	Pig (Sus)	Deer (Cervid)	Sh/Gt/ Roe	Rabbit (Oryctolagus cuniculus)
Scapula	1	1	2	-	-	-
P.humerus	4	-	1	-	-	-
D.humerus	2	1	1	-	-	-
P radius	3	4	3	1	1	-
D.radius	3	4	3	1	1	-
Ulna	-	-	-	-	-	-
P.Metacarpal	3	3	1	-	-	-
D.Metacarpal	3	5	1	-	-	-
Pelvis	3	4	-	-	-	1
P.femur	1	-	-	-	-	-
D.femur	1	-	-	-	-	-
P.tibia	14	7	1	1	-	-
D.tibia	11	7	1	1	-	-
Astragulus	-	-	1	-	-	-
Calcaneum	-	-	-	-	-	-
P.Metatarsal	3	6	1	-	-	-
D.Metatarsal	2	7	1	-	-	-
Phalanx1	2	1	-	-	-	-
Phalanx2	2	-	-	-	-	-
Phalanx3	-	-	1	-	-	-
Mandible	2	6	2	-	-	-
Tooth	2	1	1	-	-	-
Horncore	1	2	-	-	-	-
Atlas	-	-	-	-	-	-
Axis	1	-	-	-	-	-
P.Metapodial	-	1	1	-	-	-
D.Metapodial	1	1	1	-	-	-
Total	65	61	23	4	2	1
%	42	39.3	14.8	2.6	1.3	0.6

Table 19: Birds by context

Species	Context	Element
Hen (Gallus)	103	Femur
	141	Tibio-tarsus
	125	Radius
	116	Humerii (2)
Hen (Gallus)?	113	Tibio-tarsus
Goose (Anser)	120	Tibio-tarsus
	125	Tibio-tarsus
	128	Radius
	128	Carpo-metacarpus
	129	Radius
	129	Ulna
	131	Humerii (2)

Table 20: Ribs and vertebrae

Body part	Large ungulate	Small ungulate	Indeterminate
Ribs	43	19	54
Vertebrae	12	8	7
Indeterminate	6	4	77

Marine shells
by James Rackham

A few marine shells were hand excavated from the 11th to 12th-century deposits (see Table 21 below).

Freshwater and terrestrial molluscs
by James Rackham

Eight of the samples produced snail shells (Table 5) which have been identified and are summarised below (Table 22).

Only *Succinea* sp. can be classified as a terrestrial

Table 21: Frequency of valves or shells of hand-collected marine molluscs and garden snails

Context	Oyster	Mussel	Cockle	Periwinkle	Snail (*Helix aspersa*)
129	-	1	-	-	-
113	-	4	-	-	-
115	-	7	-	-	-
210	1	1	-	-	1
106	-	4	-	-	-
128	1	2	-	-	-
187	2	-	-	-	-
125	-	2	-	-	-
142	-	-	-	-	1
153	1	-	-	-	-
103	1	1	-	-	-
111	1	2	-	-	-
185	-	2	-	-	-
116	-	2	-	-	-
104	-	2	-	-	-
112	2	4	-	-	-
120	1	4	1	1	-
109	-	9	-	-	-
131	2	15	4	-	-

species, and this group includes marsh and waterside species, some of which are almost amphibious (Kerney and Cameron 1979). All of the remaining snails identified from the samples are freshwater species.

Most of these species are also characteristic of larger water bodies, rather than small pools, marshes or ditches, and some prefer running or slowly flowing water (Macan 1977; Ellis 1969). The absence of terrestrial or significant numbers of marsh or wet ground species appears significant since a lake or river margin would be expected to have an abundance of such snails around its margins. This dominance of freshwater species, characteristic of larger water bodies, indicates that Brayford Pool is likely to be the source of most of these snails; however, their low frequency in all but one sample does not imply a primary aquatic origin for the deposits. The relatively high number of shells in pit fill 125 suggests that the snails might be arriving either as a result of short flood events or from being introduced into the deposits with material collected from the Pool side, since they would not have colonised this habitat even if the pit was water-filled.

Overview and interpretation of the deposits
by James Rackham

The post-excavation analyses described above allow us to consider the questions posed in the assessment. These cover two main areas of investigation:

i   the character of the deposits and how these reflect the origins of the deposit or the function of the feature within which they lie

ii   the diet of the occupants of the site

To consider the first of these objectives, the results of the analyses are summarised in Table 23. This table has drawn on data from several areas of the analysis, both assessment and post-excavation, and presented them in different ways, primarily to allow some direct comparison between the characters of each deposit. The individual

Table 22: Freshwater and terrestrial snails identified

Context	106	125	129	153	211	172	133	210
Succinea sp.	+	-	+	-	-	1	-	-
Viviparus fasciatus	-	1	-	-	-	1	-	-
Bithynia tentaculata	-	27	-	-	1	4	-	-
Bithynia leachii	-	4	-	-	-	-	-	-
Lymnaea peregra	-	4	-	-	-	1	-	-
Lymnaea palustris	-	1	-	-	-	-	-	-
Planorbarius corneus	-	1	-	-	-	-	-	-
Planorbis planorbis	-	3	-	-	-	-	-	-
Planorbis vortex	-	11	-	+	-	2	1	+
Planorbis contortus	-	9	-	-	-	-	1	-
Planorbis leucostoma	-	1	-	-	-	-	-	-
Planorbis albus	-	3	-	-	-	-	-	-
Planorbis carinatus	-	3	-	-	-	-	-	-
Planorbis sp.	+	-	+	-	-	-	-	-
Pisidium amnicum	-	1	-	-	-	-	-	-
Pisidium sp.	-	1	-	-	-	-	-	-
Sphaerium sp.	-	-	+	-	-	-	-	-

Table 23: Summary of material in each sample taken from post-ex analysis and assessment data

Sample	12	11	9	3	14	6	10	2	13	1	4	16	17	7	18	5	8	15	19
Context	**128**	**112**	**131**	**160**	**187**	**129**	**127**	**156**	**185**	**105**	**106**	**170**	**172**	**153**	**133**	**125**	**211**	**107**	**210**
	ditch	ditch	pit	slot	ditch	pit	pit	gully	ditch	pit	layer	pit	layer	pit	ditch	pit	layer	pit	layer
Flot vol/l ml	30	37	33	45	43	17	25	31	14	42	5	8	15	5	9	11	30	23	3
Org res. v/l	111	117	292	364	143	167	175	231	45	>125	37	39	100	56	40	87	120	86	40
gravel g./10l	21	8	0	0	27	7.5	3	7	5.5	24	4	197	95	9	29	27	95	11	21
rootlets	+	+	++++	++++	+		+	+	+++		++++	++++	+++	+	+	+			
bran	++++	++++	++++	++++	++++														
apple endocarp	+++	++++	+++	++++		++	++++												
flax seeds	+++	+++	+++	++++		+++	+												
straw?	+++	+++	++++	++++	++	+++	++++	++		++				+		++			
moss	++++	+++	+++	++	++++	++++	+++	++	++	+	+	+	+++	+		+		+	
heathers	+++	+++	+++	++	++	++++	++++	+						++				++	+
Charcoal rich``	+		o	o		+			+	o				o	+		+		+
eggshell	+			+					+						+		+		++
Aquatic sn.						+					+	+	+	+		+++	+		
Daphnia	+++	++	++			++		+++	+++++	++	++++	++	++	+++++	+++		+++		++
Caddis															+	+			
Leach egg													+			+			
Freshw. fish		1	1			2			1	1	3						3		
Marine fish		3				1	2		3	1	2				2		3	1	1
Bone g./10l	74	62	73	67	35	31	74	15	3	13	18	0	47	13	11	56	47	6	43
Shell g./10l	30	17	8	3	47	35	9	7	7	7	10	+	73	4	18	1	13	3	18
Char'dplant																			
Cereal/30 l.	14.4	21	5	5.4	5	12.5	10.5	2.3	9.5	6.2	12.3		2.5	3.3	21	65.2	>30	8.6	>30
Wood	*12*	*11*	*9*	*3*	*14*	*6*	*10*	*2*	*13*	*1*					*18*		*8*		
Sliver/chip	+	+	+	+	+	+	+			+					+				
Pos. heather							++												
Min wood	+	+	+	+															

Table 23 (cont.): Summary of material in each sample taken from post-ex analysis and assessment data

Sample	12	11	9	3	14	6	10	2	13	1	4	16	17	7	18	5	8	15	19
Context	**128**	**112**	**131**	**160**	**187**	**129**	**127**	**156**	**185**	**105**	**106**	**170**	**172**	**153**	**133**	**125**	**211**	**107**	**210**
	ditch	ditch	pit	slot	ditch	pit	pit	gully	ditch	pit	layer	pit	layer	pit	ditch	pit	layer	pit	layer
Wat. Plants																			
Weeds	49	43	44	50	43	57	60.5	50	63.5	68.5	48	50	57	48.5	38.5	44			
Waste	47.5	48	**58.5**	**61.5**	48.5	**57**	**58**	**55.5**	**72.5**	**71.5**	**61**	**54**	**57**	**57.5**	48	47			
Woods	42.5	39	41.5	41	34	37	37	50	41	37	39	37.5	43	36	29	35			
Open	41	34	34	34	31.5	45	37	55.5	36	48.5	42	46	38	42.5	35.5	41			
Wet	38	37.5	41.5	32	46	43	35	**66.5**	45.5	43	45	**75**	**54**	**54.5**	**61**	**62**			
Edible	36	37.5	41.5	43	34	29.5	25.5	22	41	26	26	21	40.5	27	32	35			
Medical	34	32	32	34	43	33.5	35	39	45.5	43	32	25	32.5	30	26	23.5			
Industrial	26	25	29	27	28.5	31.5	28	28	45.5	26	19	33	30	27	29	26.5			
Cultivated	**20**	**16**	**17**	**18**	8.5	10	11.5	0	13.5	0	3	4	5	0	6.5	9			
Total taxa	*61*	*56*	*41*	*44*	*35*	*51*	*43*	*18*	*22*	*35*	*31*	*24*	*37*	*33*	*31*	*34*			
Insects	**12**	**11**	**9**	**3**	**14**	**6**	**10**	**2**	**13**	**1**			**17**						
aquatic	0	2.4	2.5	1	0	0	10.3	6.5	9.5	33			17.5						
Waterside/banks	9.8	1.2	1.5	1	10	0	2.6	0	0	0			0						
Oa*	34	27	26	38	42.5	22	41	20	9.5	67			29						
House	6.6	2.4	4	1.8	10	2.4	**17.9**	**23.9**	**28.6**	0			0						
S synan	4.9	2.4	0	0	0	2.4	5.1	17.4	14.3	0			0						
Foul/dung	13.1	15.4	24.2	39	30	14.6	0	4.3	0	0			6						
Cess assoc*	++	++	++	+++		+													
Total indiv	*61*	*84*	*198*	*162*	*40*	*41*	*39*	*46*	*21*	*3*			*17*						
Parasites	**12**	**11**	**9**	**3**		**6**				**1**									
Trichurid	+	++	++	++										7					
Ascaris	+	+	+	+															

* see Table 5 for key

components of the assemblage are either quantified in a broad manner, presented as percentages of the total identified assemblage, or as a plain numerical frequency or frequency per volume of sediment.

Character of deposits

The identification in the assessment report (Rackham 2001) of four of the deposits, 128, 112, 131 and 160 as containing cess is confirmed by the analyses. These contexts specifically show high concentrations of cereal bran, flax seeds and apple endocarp fragments; cultivated and edible plants (waterlogged) are more abundant in these samples than the others and insects associated with cess deposits are common. All four produced the ova of parasitic trichurid and ascarid worms, probably those parasitic in both humans and pigs. There is also a strong association of straw (?) and moss with these deposits. The straw might derive from animal bedding and could account for the presence of pig parasitic worm ova, or straw may have been used to cover over the cess deposits, or perhaps even derive from discarded bedding from human habitation or floor covering. The moss, and perhaps also the straw, may have been used as contemporary toilet paper. Kenward and Hall (1995) suggest the use of mosses for anal wipes at Coppergate. The mineralised condition of much of the wood in the deposits is probably also a product of the concentration of cess. These deposits contain material from a variety of other sources including domestic rubbish, small amounts of wood-working debris and seeds and insects from the local flora and fauna. They also represent the 'richest' assemblages in terms of species diversity. While it is reasonable to conclude that pit 144 in the centre of the site was probably a cesspit or latrine, two of the samples derive from ditch 191 and one from 'slot' 140. Both upper and lower fills of ditch 191 (112 and 128) towards the southern end of the trench are so clearly dominated by elements deriving from, or indicating, cess that it must be concluded that this feature is a primary or direct secondary receptacle for human faecal waste, and on the basis of the parasite eggs presumably also pig bedding. It may be that latrines were set up over the ditch or waste from elsewhere was dumped in it. Slot 140 (context 160), a narrow feature only 0.3m wide but 7m long seems an unexpected feature to contain faecal deposits. A piece of degraded timber was found near one end and it appears that this was a timber slot that probably contained a plank (Taylor 2001). The assemblages are very similar to the other cess-rich features although they lack the apple endocarp fragments and have a marked foul rotting matter or dung insect assemblage. It is difficult to reconcile a cess deposit with a feature that might have contained a large oak radially split heartwood plank but if this was the floor of a wooden trough or drain it might have formed a 'drain' within a structure where animals were stalled or been associated with a human latrine.

There are three other deposits that have produced similar assemblages to these cess-rich deposits, but lack any clear evidence for the presence of parasite ova (where these have been studied), produced no mineralised wood, and had lower densities of cess-associated insects and cultivated plants. These are contexts 187, 129 and 127 from ditch 188, pit 157 and pit 146 respectively. Bran is abundant in 187, with some flax seeds and straw (?) and has a high foul rotting matter and dung insect assemblage. Contexts 129 and 127 lack the bran, but 127 includes apple endocarp fragments, while they both contain flax seeds, straw and moss. Context 127 lacks any insect taxa classified as foul rotting matter and dung species, but does include a high 'house' fauna. Contexts 129 and 127 both include lots of well preserved heather shoots and capsules, while 127 also includes much twiggy material, probably also of heather. Ditch 187 runs parallel with and predates the cess-rich ditch 191 and it is probable that it had a similar function. Some input of cess is evident although a high outdoor insect fauna and foul rotting matter and dung fauna combined with a very mixed plant seed assemblage might suggest a more open environment at this time (Phase 2, 11th – 12th centuries). Context 127 contains a high outdoor insect assemblage and a high weed and waste ground plant seed assemblage, but the high 'house' insect fauna component suggests that domestic waste from within a building is being dumped in the pit, along with more general rubbish including bone and shell. This pit also produced a spindle-whorl and a possible hammerstone, both suggestive of rubbish from a house. The heather present in this sample and several of the others already discussed must have been imported to the site, since the local ground conditions are completely unsuitable for its growth. Heather has a variety of uses including firelighters, fuel, fodder, thatch, basket work, rope, packing, bedding (including human), dye, tea and beer flavouring (Mabey 1996). In these contexts it is perhaps as likely to derive from bedding as any others and its positive association with evidence for cess (Table 18) and its predominantly waterlogged condition, although charred capsules are also present in ditch 188, appears to reflect its domestic use for things other than fuel. All these cess rich samples tend to have the highest concentrations of domestic animal bone, and to a lesser extent edible marine shell indicating the incorporation of ordinary domestic food waste, but none show any evidence for more concentrated dumping.

Four contexts (comprising 185, 106, 170 and 172) produced much lower levels of organic debris and much smaller floats, the latter dominated by small fibrous rootlets. Such rootlets are often a problem with deposits that fall within the range of recent plants growing on the ground surface, but at this site these deposits are fairly well sealed and with two samples from deposits above producing very few rootlets, but still containing well preserved organic remains, these roots appear likely to reflect evidence for an ancient ground surface above them. The relative absence of an insect fauna (see above) typical of open ground in contexts 172 and 185 need not conflict with this interpretation if the ground surface was above the sampled deposit. The generally poorer preservation, lower species diversity and smaller flots are consistent with a deposit that was biologically active, while the greater content of gravel in 170 and 172 reflects the much greater mineral component in these deposits. Context 172 is described as a levelling layer and occurs at the base of the archaeological sequence at the north end of the trench. This area of the site is likely to have been reclaimed from the marshy margins of the Brayford Pool earliest and this and the Phase 2 pit (context 170 in pit 203) a few metres south both include a significant aquatic and wetland plant element, with 172 having the highest aquatic insect component. All these samples also include appreciable numbers of *Daphnia* (water flea) ephippia, some have freshwater snails and 172 also produced leach eggs. All these indicate a strong freshwater element and despite clear evidence for 11th or 12th-century activity on the site it is likely that it was subject to seasonal flooding when the water level in the Pool rose.

The initial study and dating of the natural sediments underlying the archaeological sequence suggest a period of drying out during the Saxon period with downslope movement of sands from the terrestrial environment to the north being interleaved with waterlain sediments deposited by the Pool. Context 172 might well have its origin as a slopewash sand mixed with organic deposits forming on the margins of the Pool, which could explain the presence of Roman material in it, while the archaeologial debris in all the later layers is almost certainly *in situ*. Context 172 lies about 0.4m below the level from which the early features at this end of the trench are cut, but still has a few sherds of mid to late 11th-century pottery indicating that it had already formed by the late 11th century. The ground surface contemporary with the excavation of the first features on the site was therefore above 172 and could easily have been the vegetated surface responsible for the rootlets in the sample. In 106, 185 and 170 the rootlets must reflect the development of vegetated ground surfaces within the archaeological sequence, particularly since two of these layers are pit fills. The highest proportion of insects classifiable into the 'house' fauna category in context 185 suggests rubbish from habitation entering the deposits or proximity to buildings, but functionally this ditch, 186, seems likely to reflect the southern boundary of the occupation on the north shore of the Brayford at this time, much as the two earlier ditches 191 and 188 probably did. The Phase 2 ditch 188 at the southern end of the trench shows no greater proportion of aquatic and waterside plants and insects than many other samples, and produced relatively few *Daphnia* ephippia, and this first ditch dug at the south end of the trench may have been excavated and filled during a period of relatively low water level in the Pool. The fill of pit 203 is relatively lacking in archaeological finds of any sort and with the highest gravel content and one of the lowest organic contents this fill of cut 203 is largely mineral in character. It may have been filled by downslope wash deposits or back-filled with local sands and silts.

The aquatic element present in the deposits discussed above is also present in three more samples (contexts 153, 133 and 125). These all produced a high wetland plant component. they also included *Daphnia* ephippia, freshwater snails, caddis larval cases and leach eggs. While this material may have entered the deposits with vegetation collected from a waterside environment, the consistency of this aquatic element does seem to suggest that the area was still subject to flooding in phase 5. The freshwater mollusc fauna in 125 is indicative of a large water body such as the Pool and not a ditch or waterfilled pit environment and the concentration of shells in this deposit might suggest either a flood strand line deposit or the dumping of material such as reeds collected from the margins of the Pool.

Diet

Because of the excellent state of preservation of plant remains and clear evidence for several deposits containing cess or latrine waste we can obtain rather more information on the early medieval diet at this site than would normally be possible for contemporary sites in Lincoln. While a considerable number of the plants that have been identified do have potential as food and records indicate that they have been eaten, it would be naïve to assume that all such plants were eaten at this site. In order to get some handle on which plants may have been eaten the edible plants are listed in Table 24 and the frequency with which they occurred in the seven samples containing evidence for cess has been compared with their frequency in the nine other samples from which the plant remains were studied. Some of these are genera or groups and it is not certain whether the seeds include the edible taxa or not. Plant taxa that are ubiquitous, occurring in most samples from both types are likely to be those generally contributing to the local seed bank, and although it cannot be ruled out that they were eaten, it is probable that they represent the local flora on the site. Those that occur proportionally in both sample sets are also likely to be representatives of the local flora. One or two species such as the grasses and heathers may be selectively present in the 'cess' samples because of factors other than diet, such as selective disposal of material being used elsewhere or even as 'toilet paper'. This leaves a set of taxa which are clearly good eating and occur in several of the cess samples, and those which occur much more frequently in the cess samples suggesting that their concentration in these samples may be related to concentrations of cess in the samples.

Of the good fruits and berries, bramble/raspberry is perhaps surprisingly under-represented in the cess deposits and in no samples were they abundant, perhaps suggesting that these were part of the local flora rather than regular food items. However, a group of plant taxa including wild carrot, wild parsnip, mallow, hawkbit, black bindweed, *Apium* (wild celery or fool's water cress), nipplewort and bogbean occur in the cess samples, either exclusively or with much greater freqency than the other samples and this association suggests that they may have been intentionally eaten or incorporated with the cereals which were eaten. In addition to these species a few plant species have some medicinal qualities. These are presented in Table 25 (in the same manner as Table 24) and, apart from those that are also edible, woundwort, self-heal and bryony occur only in the cess pit samples, although in each case it is not the seeds but the root or leaves that are used for medicinal purposes. Other taxa including the knapweeds, stinking mayweed and thorow-wax occur with much greater frequency in the cess samples but all may have been introduced as weeds with the cereals or the straw. The other taxa show no specific concentration and probably reflect the general flora of the area.

Wild plants, therefore, almost certainly exploited for food include sloe, bullace, hazelnut, bramble and elderberry, although the latter two show no concentration in the cess deposits. It is possible that wild carrot, wild parsnip, mallow, hawkbit and black bindweed were also used

Table 24: Frequency of samples in which each identified food taxa was recorded

		Cess samples *(7)*	*Other samples* *(9)*
CHARRED			
Bread/club wheat	*Triticum aestivo-compactum*	4	2
Wheat	*Tritcum* sp.	1	2
Barley	*Hordeum vulgare*	6	4
Rye	*Secale cereale*	1	-
Oats	*Avena* sp.	6	7
Tare, vetchling, pea	*Vicia/Lathyrus/Pisum*	-	1
Heather	*Calluna vulgaris*	2	-
WATERLOGGED		-	-
Cereal bran	Cerealia indet	5	-
Flax	*Linum usitatissimum*	7	-
Sloe	*Prunus spinosa*	4	1
Plum/bullace	*Prunus domestica*	4	1
Cherry	*Prunus avium*	3	-
Apple/crab	*Malus domestica/sylvestris*	4	-
Apple/crab endocarp	*Malus domestica/sylvestris*	4	-
Apple/pear	*Pyrus/Malus* sp.	2	-
Hazelnut	*Corylus avellana*	7	2
Bramble/raspberry	*Rubus fruticosus/ideaus*	2	3
Elderberry	*Sambucus nigra*	6	9
Possible food plants		-	-
Wild carrot	*Daucus carota*	2	-
Wild parsnip	*Pastinaca sativa*	2	-
Mallow	*Malva sylvestris*	2	-
Hawkbit	*Leontodon* sp.	4	1
Black bindweed	*Fallopia convolvulus*	5	1
Wild celery/fools water cress	*Apium* sp	3	2
Grasses	Gramineae	5	2
Nipplewort	*Lapsana communis*	5	2
Heather/ling	*Calluna vulgaris*	6	1
Bogbean	*Menyanthes trifoliata*	6	3
Cabbage family	*Brassica/Sinapsis* spp.	3	4
Cinquefoil/tormentil	*Potentilla* sp.	3	5
Campion/catchfly	*Silene* spp.	3	6
Knotgrasses/persicarias	*Polygonum* spp.	4	3
Stinging nettle	*Urtica dioica*	4	6
Docks	*Rumex* spp.	5	5
Black nightshade	*Solanum nigrum*	5	6
Goosefoots	*Chenopodium* spp.	6	8
Orache	*Atriplex* spp.	7	8
Poppy	*Papaver* spp.	-	1
Mint	*Mentha* sp.	-	2

Table 24 (cont.): Frequency of samples in which each identified food taxa was recorded

		Cess samples (7)	Other samples (9)
Picked from residue		*(7)*	*(12)*
Mussel	*Mytilus edulis*	7	11
Cockle	*Cardium edule*	5	6
Oyster	*Ostrea edulis*	5	4
Periwinkle	*Littorina littorea*	2	3
Whelk		1	-
Eel	*Anguilla anguilla*	-	2
Herring	*Clupea harengus*	-	4
Pike	*Esox lucius*	2	2
Roach	*Rutilus rutilus*	-	1
Cod	*Gadus morhua*	3	1
Small gadid	Gadidae	-	1
Large gadid	Gadidae	2	3
Perch	*Perca fluviatilis*	2	-
Cattle		5	7
Sheep		6	7
Pig		6	5
Goose, domestic		1	2
Chicken		2	1
Bird eggshell		2	4
Wild bird	Not identified	-	1

although only the seeds of the latter are used as food, while leaves and roots of the other plants are the food item. Cultivated fruits are suggested by apple/crab apple, apple/pear, plums and cherry, although both the cherry and apples could be wild varieties. Significant differences in the plum stones suggest that more than one variety was available. Cultivated crops include bread/club wheat, barley, oats, rye and flax, the abundance of seeds of the latter in the cess deposits suggesting that these were a food item, perhaps on or in the bread that might be represented by the large quantities of bran in the samples. There is evidence that flax was being pressed for oil in the Norse period in Ireland (Dickson and Dickson 2000) and the seeds can be used as a laxative. Although seeds can fall from flax stems hung up to dry after retting, the absence of capsules in these samples would argue against linen fibre production as the origin of these seeds. Oats and barley occur in the greatest number of samples and with the greatest individual frequency, suggesting these were probably the most important cereals.

The quantity of bran in several of the samples is high and although this is currently presumed to be the surviving fragments of coarse ground cereal from bread, or possibly a porridge (Dickson and Dickson 2000), it remains possible that it could derive from a mash discarded after fermentation. None of the charred cereal showed any evidence of germination, but its density was very low and it probably had a different origin to the bran. If the

bran was derived from a mash used in brewing then it is possible that the heather may also have had this role. Heather ale is known in the recent past to have been produced from the tops of heather shoots mixed with malt and a few hops (Mabey 1996) and has an ancient tradition in Scotland. This remains an alternative explanation for the association of heather and bran in several samples but bedding is probably a simpler interpretation for the heather.

These taxa are likely to represent only a proportion of the different plants used as food, since most of those plants whose vegetative parts are eaten, such as root crops, bulbs and leaf crops are unlikely to leave any identifiable trace even in these well preserved deposits.

A range of animal foods was picked from the residues of the samples, but in such organic rich deposits these occur at much lower densities than many non-organic deposits. The local fish resources from the Brayford Pool and the Rivers Witham and Till (or Fosdyke) that ran into the Pool appear to have afforded catches of pike, roach, perch and eel. These are the more common taxa recorded by Irving (Dobney *et al* 1994) from deposits in Lincoln. Even at this date marine fish were probably more important than freshwater taxa, and nearly 63% of the identified fish species in this small sample are marine fish. These include herring and cod, with several bones of large and small gadids that have not been identified

Table 25: Frequency of samples with seeds of plants with medicinal qualities

No. samples		Cess rich 7	others 9
Woundwort	*Stachys sp.*	1	-
Wild carrot	*Daucus carota*	2	-
Cherry	*Prunus avium*	3	-
Self-heal	*Prunella vulgaris*	3	-
White bryony	*Bryonia dioica*	4	-
Thorow-wax	*Bupleurum rotundifolium*	3	1
Sloe	*Prunus spinosa*	4	1
Cornflower	*Centaurea cyanus*	4	1
Knapweeds	*Centaurea spp.*	7	1
Thistles	*Carduus/Cirsium spp.*	5	2
Stinking mayweed	*Anthemis cotula*	7	2
Bogbean	*Menyanthes trifoliata*	6	3
Common knapweed	*Centaurea nigra*	1	1
Lesser spearwort	*Ranunculus flammula*	2	1
Chickweed/stichwort	*Stellaria spp.*	2	1
Bramble/raspberry	Rubus fruticosus/ideaus	2	3
Cabbage family	*Brassica/ Sinapsis spp.*	3	4
Violet	*Viola spp.*	3	5
Cinquefoil/tormentil	*Potentilla spp.*	3	5
Knotgrasses, persicarias	*Polygonum spp.*	4	3
Stinging nettle	*Urtica dioica*	4	6
Docks	*Rumex spp.*	5	5
Knotgrass	*Polygonum aviculare*	6	4
White horehound	*Maribium vulgare*	6	5
Elderberry	*Sambucus nigra*	6	9
Buttercups	*Ranunculus acris/repens/bulbosus*	7	8
Orache	*Atriplex spp.*	7	8
Poppy	*Papaver spp.*	-	1
Henbane	*Hyoscyanus niger*	-	2
Mint	*Mentha spp.*	-	2

to species. These bones clearly reflect the trading of sea fish to the city, almost certainly up the Witham from Boston, a trade which may have been undertaken with the shellfish that were found. They occur with a greater frequency than the fishes. The latter include mussels, cockles, oysters, periwinkles and whelks, with mussels being the most common, both in the samples, occurring in all but one of the nineteen samples, and also in the hand-collected assemblage. Shellfish in their shells have to be traded alive and these may have been a frequently consumed food at the site.

The bulk of the meat eaten at the site will have been from domestic animals, and cattle, sheep, pig, chicken and goose bones were identified from the soil samples. Sheep occurred in one more sample than cattle, which broadly agrees with the hand-collected bone assemblage in which sheep and cattle bones occur in similar numbers (Deighton, this report; Table 18), although cattle and

cattle-size bones were a bit more abundant, probably due to their greater chances of recovery during the excavation process. Pig bones were much less frequent in the hand-collected sample, but were present in only one less soil sample than cattle, and may have been more important than the excavated sample suggests. Goose and chicken bones were found in many fewer samples and in smaller numbers in the excavated sample, with the latter suggesting that goose was probably a more important meat source, although chickens may have been the main producer of any eggs that were eaten at the site, shells of which were recorded from six samples. Two species were identified among the excavated bones that did not appear in the samples, a rabbit bone, probably from one of the later contexts, and four bones assigned to a cervid (deer).

These assemblages are inappropriate for assigning any relative contribution of the different food items but they do give a fairly good indication of the range of taxa available to and consumed at the site.

In general these deposits were not as rich in fish and mammal bone as many contemporary urban deposits are in towns such as Kings Lynn and Boston, and further afield. This may be due to a comparatively low incidence of general domestic rubbish in the deposits at this location, or perhaps because of the large volume of organic debris surviving in the features fills there has been less concentration of the non-organic rubbish.

Crafts

There are a few small indications that crafts may have been undertaken on or near the site, but nothing conclusive. The presence of small quantities of hammerscale in two of the samples, some probably smithing slag, and a possible small iron billet in ditch fill 187 (Hylton, this report, SF3) indicate that iron smithing was occurring somewhere in the vicinity. These concentrations are low and the activity must have been taking place beyond the limits of the excavation trench. The occurrence of small chips and shavings of roundwood and timber in several of the samples indicates local woodworking on the site. These do not occur with great frequency and they probably derived from small scale construction activity associated with buildings, fences and hurdles that may have been made and erected on the plot. It is possible that the heather shoots recorded in several samples could

derive from dyeing, but with such a range of uses for this species, as Kenward and Hall have noted (1995), it is not possible to be certain that dyeing was one of its roles at this site. While we have argued that the flax was derived from food remains the presence of stem fragments that might include flax in three samples raises the possibility that some of the features may have been used for retting, a suggestion which we cannot unfortunately confirm on the evidence collected.

Kenward and Hall's (1995) work at Coppergate suggested that the deposits at the back of the tenement plots were those that contained most of the cess deposits. It may be that the distribution of cess rich deposits within the southern half of the trench, and particularly in two of the ditches at the southern end that may mark the boundary of the plot/plots that were excavated, suggests that the excavation trench lies in the southern 'back' part of tenements facing onto Newlands to the north. The presence of parasites probably derived from pigs suggests that these, and possibly other animals, may have been kept in this 'back yard' area of the tenement. The wetland elements in the samples probably relate to conditions in the ditches and flood events, possibly seasonal, or active collection of waterside plants or even water, rather than strand line accumulations around the edge of the Pool. The Brayford end of these plots is likely to have been a fairly useless damp boggy area, probably prone to flooding at this time, and the development of the Pool side as a dock or wharf area probably post-dates this activity.

Chapter 5: General Discussion

In conjunction with the evidence gathered from earlier archaeological investigations in the area, the evidence gained from the excavation in June 2000 has provided an enhanced insight into land use and the local environment on the north bank of Brayford Pool, spanning a period from the late Bronze Age through to the 12th century AD. It is of particular interest in terms of the expansion of the medieval town to the south of the Roman city wall from the 11th century onwards in the area that later became known as *Baxtergate*. However, the relatively small area covered by the excavation limits the detailed structural interpretation of many of the medieval features and provides more of a general picture of land use along this stretch of the waterfront at this time. Sites referred to in the following discussion are shown in Figure 20.

Prehistoric and Roman deposits

The earliest environmental evidence came from two boreholes sunk at either end of the trench. The cores revealed a sequence of deposits overlying alluvial sands, commencing with the development of a thick, woody peat bed in the late Bronze Age. The peat deposits are indicative of a marginal aquatic environment of reeds and grasses, probably developing into a fen carr type habitat at the Pool margins. Such an environment would typically have been dominated by trees, for example birch (*Betula pubescens*), alder (*Alnus glutinosa*) and ash (*Fraxinus excelsior*), with an under-storey of fen herbs and ferns (Walker 1970).

The inception of peat growth may have been entirely due to natural circumstances, such as changes in the hydrological regime of the local rivers brought about by sea-level fluctuation, but it is possible that human activity may have played some part in the development of the peat beds. This is hinted at by the recovery of high quality metalwork of late Bronze Age and Iron Age date in the River Witham at Stamp End, less than a kilometre downstream from Brayford Pool (Davey 1971; 1973; White 1979). This assemblage of artefacts, which includes swords, axes and spearheads, conforms to the group of items typically placed as 'votive' offerings in rivers, lakes and pools in the 1st millennium BC. Such 'votive' deposits are often associated with a causeway, such as that discovered at Flag Fen (Pryor 2001) and Fiskerton (Field 1986), and it has been suggested that a causeway may have existed at Stamp End in the prehistoric period (Jones and Stocker 2003).

The case for a causeway at Stamp End in the prehistoric period is given further support by the topography of the Witham valley in this area. Prior to the construction of the Roman crossing over the River Witham at Wigford, the narrowest and most convenient point to cross the river was in the vicinity of Stamp End, where spurs of higher ground approach the river on both banks, above the level of the marshes. It is therefore likely that in the prehistoric period the river would have been crossed at this point, a crossing that may have been augmented by the construction of a timber causeway. Such a structure, even if it had stopped at the main channel, would have acted as a barrier during times of flooding and may have altered the flow of the river upstream at Brayford Pool, creating an environment suitable for the development of peat beds in this locality.

Overlying the woody peat was a layer of fibrous peat, which continued to accumulate until around the late 7th to 9th centuries AD when the ground appears to have dried out sufficiently to begin to attract settlement along the Pool edge. The change in the structure and composition of the peat indicates a marked change in the local habitat, most likely from fen carr back to an environment of sandy islets surrounded by brackish pools and rivulets, the vegetation dominated by reeds and grasses. When this change occurred is uncertain, but based on the rate of accumulation of the peat, it is likely to have occurred in the late prehistoric or Roman period. It is possible that the change may be associated with the establishment of the Roman waterfront and 'hard' in the second half of the 1st century AD, initially created to serve the Roman military occupation of the area and later the *colonia*. This could have involved the deliberate clearance of the fen carr to create a more open approach to the foreshore, or the water level in the Pool could have been artificially controlled by the construction of dams and weirs in the vicinity of Stamp End. Jones (2003, 99-101) suggests that such a water-control system may have been constructed in the late 3rd or early 4th century as a response to natural changes in the hydrology of the river, and to enable the construction of a quayside.

The 'hard' occupied the sloping foreshore below the south wall of the lower City and extended at least 50m to the south of the wall. This would approximately place the shoreline across the northern end of the excavation trench. It is interesting to note that the fibrous peat in the core taken from the north end of the trench was interdigitated with lenses of sand, probably washed down from the sloping foreshore and into the shallow waters at the edge of the Pool. The sand lenses could be associated with ground disturbance and activity along the 'hard' during the Roman period, with possible waterfront activity continuing along the foreshore through to the medieval period.

Medieval occupation

Aside from the tantalising evidence for earlier activity revealed in the two cores referred to above, the archaeological remains generally dated to the 11th and 12th centuries; later remains had been destroyed by modern development. The medieval remains consisted of several ditches and gullies, a possible timber building, a line of

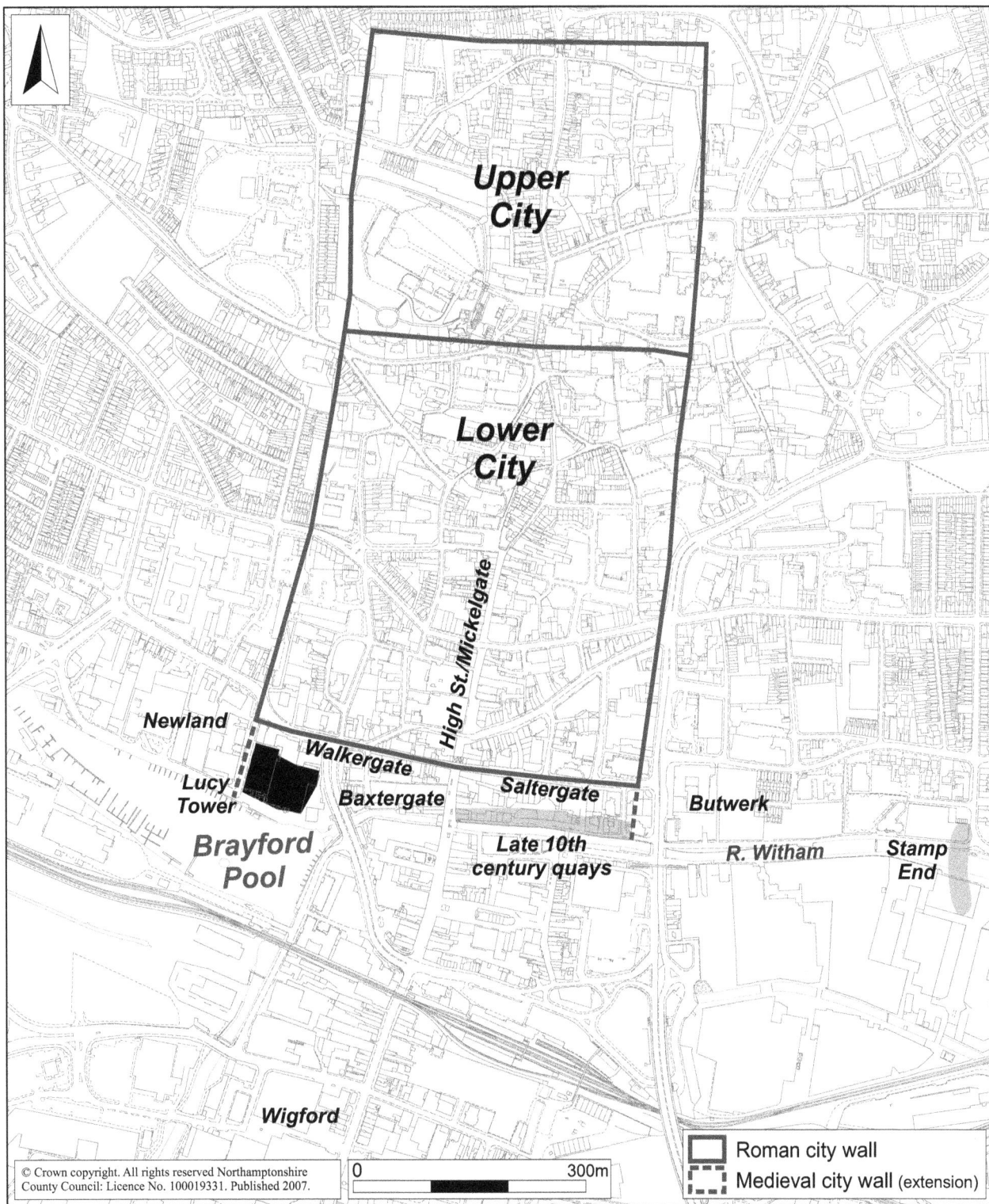

Fig 20: Brayford Pool and the City of Lincoln

timber stakes, perhaps a wattle fence, and rubbish and cess pits, interspersed with sequences of laid deposits. The features and deposits are typical of 'backyard' activity, probably to the rear of buildings located to the north of the trench.

Before discussing the medieval remains in detail, a brief overview of the medieval topography of the southern suburb will assist in understanding the site in its wider

context. The site lies within an important area of the city that is poorly understood in terms of its medieval past; the handful of archaeological investigations that have been undertaken in the area have often been small and have been carried out under less than favourable conditions. In the medieval period the site lay within the suburb that developed on the narrow strip of land to the south of the city wall, extending down to the shoreline of Brayford Pool. The name of the suburb has been identified from documents as *Baxtergate*, a name which originally may have begun as a street name, the 'street of bakers', but was later used for the suburb (Vince 2003, 240). Until the development of quays and water-control systems to the east, near Stamp End, and the increasing use of the 'hard' at Wigford, the foreshore would have served as a port for the city, and would have been occupied by warehouses, sheds and slipways, as well as houses. Initally there was a 'hard', which was probably developed into a quay in the late 10th century, at least to the east of High Street. There is currently no clear evidence for an upright quay to the west of High Street prior to the second half of the 13th century. The suburb was probably enclosed to the east and west by the southern continuation of the city ditch, which would have opened out into Brayford Pool. In the late 13th or early 14th centuries the city wall was extended down to the waterfront and into the river, with gates to the east and west providing access to the extra-mural suburbs of *Butwerk* and *Newland* respectively. The Lucy Tower was built at the southern terminal of the western extension. Leading from Newland Gate in the west, a thoroughfare, probably called *Walkergate*, ran eastwards towards High Street, and continued to the east of High Street as *Saltergate*, terminating at Staple Place. A gateway led out of Staple Place into the suburb of *Butwerk*. This east to west thoroughfare was either built over or lay immediately to the south of the old Roman city wall. High Street followed the line of Ermine Street, crossing High Bridge to the suburb of Wigford on the south bank.

Having considered the general topography of the medieval suburb and waterfront of *Baxtergate*, it is clear that the medieval remains from the present excavations are of considerable interest in terms of the development of the medieval city. The earliest deposits are a sequence of layers, which probably date to the mid/late 11th century, overlying what was probably the foreshore prior to the gradual development of this strip of land south of the city wall. The foreshore deposit contained some environmental evidence to suggest that settlement waste was being deposited here, but the environmental picture is generally of a marginal aquatic environment, with water-borne organic material washed up on the strand, mixing with slopewash. The settlement waste may have been dumped directly onto the foreshore, with additional flotsam being washed up at times of high water levels, having entered the Pool from the city ditch, or from some other outlet. With the exception of one layer, which produced a small quantity of pottery sherds of mid/late 11th to mid 12th-century date, the overlying layers produced few finds, and it is likely that they represent attempts to reclaim land along the Pool margins, or efforts to stabilise the foreshore against erosion. Such activity suggests that there may have been some form of settlement in the vicinity at this time, perhaps associated with the continued use of the foreshore as a 'hard'.

Towards the end of the 11th century and perhaps as late as the mid 12th century, the foreshore appears to have been formally divided into plots, their southern edge defined by ditches running parallel to the shoreline. The excavated area was, however, too limited to determine the size of any of these plots. The ditches, which run parallel and to the north of the walls and timber piles discovered

during excavations in 1975, appear to have been open for some time and contained foul rotting matter, dung and faecal waste, indicative of more permanent settlement in the immediate area. Subsequent pit digging, generally associated with the disposal of foul and domestic waste, appears to be largely confined to the north of these ditches. These and the later deposits of settlement refuse contained abundant and exceptional evidence for early medieval diet. As well as the commonly occurring barley and oats, this appears to have included flax, and a variety of wild fruits such as plums, cherries, crab apples hazelnuts and blackberries. Wild food plants such as carrot and parsnip may also have been intentionally gathered. Freshwater fish (pike, roach, eel), shellfish (especially mussels, cockles and oysters), and sea fish, such as herring and cod, were eaten. Meat from the the common domesticates – cow, sheep and pig – was common, along with chickens and their eggs.

The foreshore was probably still open at this time as the area still appears to have been periodically flooded and the plant and insect remains are indicative of an open, wetland environment. The slope of the deposits towards the Pool also suggests that a formal quayside had yet to be established; the area behind any quay would presumably have been built up and levelled had it been in existence at this time.

Broadly of the same period but sealing the pits and ditches mentioned above, there was a reasonably thick layer of soil (*c* 0.35m thick) extending across the entire trench. The organic component of this soil horizon was highly degraded, indicating that it had been biologically active, and the presence of plant rootlets suggests that it had a vegetated surface. There is little indication that the land was used for cultivation or for any other purpose, so it is likely that it may have been waste ground for a period of time.

Following the apparent hiatus in activity on the site, activity recommenced at some point during the mid to late 12th century with the excavation of four sub-rectangular, steep-sided, flat-bottomed pits or slots. They lay parallel to each other, terminated in a line, had relatively clean sandy fills and were spaced between 1.2m and 2.2m apart. They are unlikely to be ditch terminals as they were not found in the trench excavated immediately to the west in 1975. The purpose of these pits or slots is uncertain, and interpretation is not aided by the fact that they had been truncated and extended beyond the confines of the trench. It is possible that they may have been the footings of a timber building, perhaps a shed, with timber ring beams set directly on the ground surface over the compacted sandy fill of the foundation trenches. Pits excavated inside this tentative building appear to lie between the footings, perhaps respecting internal partitions, and one of the pits was rich in cess, in sufficient concentrations to suggest that it may have been used as a latrine pit. A possible beam slot, still containing remnants of an oak plank, lay across the eastern side of the northernmost 'cell' of the building, suggesting that it may have been open-sided and that it was later blocked in. The slot contained animal dung and foul rotting matter, so it is possible that the building served as an animal byre, at least in this later phase of use. Although this feature might be interpreted as a drain or soakaway, this seems unlikely as it had no point of discharge.

Aligned from east to west and running alongside the possible building mentioned above was a gully or ditch, which may have served as a plot boundary or subdivision, or as a drain. The ditch contained standing water, at least seasonally, and it appeared to have been partly re-cut or cleaned out in places. Once it had silted up a spread of cobbles was laid down over a small area, perhaps to consolidate a trampled, wet patch of ground in a hollow left by the ditch or to provide an area of hard standing for a trough.

Towards the end of the 12th century (Phase 7) a phase of land reclamation took place. Here, a thick deposit, comprising two silty layers with a combined thickness of c 0.5m, built up over the previous land surface over a relatively short period of time, too short a period to allow for natural accumulation. The layers, which were reasonably homogeneous, contained domestic waste, including broken pottery, the ashes from domestic fires and dumps of mortar; the remains of wooden stakes and a post suggest that the made-ground may have been secured in place with wattle hurdles, although this is not certain. There was some evidence for pit digging in the raised land surface, and for a further layer of made-ground, although none of this later activity produced any dating evidence. Due to modern destruction of the later medieval deposits, the subsequent development of the site is unknown. However, this reclamation appears to have laid the foundation for the construction of quays following the late 13th or early 14th-century extension of the city wall to the Lucy Tower.

This would seem to mirror, at a later date, the situation to the east of High Street, below *Saltergate*. Here, a thick deposit of river silt and domestic rubbish, held in place by a lattice of wicker hurdles, built up during the late 10th and 11th centuries behind the late 10th-century quayside (Vince 2003, 237).

To conclude, it appears that during the medieval period, at least up until the end of the 12th century, the stretch of waterfront to the west of High Street was probably used as a 'hard', situated to the west of the late 10th-century quayside below *Saltergate*. Sparsely occupied in the Late Saxon period, the expansion of the city in the Saxo-Norman period led to increased settlement and activity along this stretch of the waterfront, with residential properties, sheds and slipways being built. It is likely that commercial vessels would have used the facilities at the quays to the east, and the 'hard' was probably only used by local fishermen and by people whose premises backed on to the Pool. The risk of flooding, and the generally damp conditions along the Pool margins, would have made this area a fairly insalubrious neighbourhood prior to the extension of the quayside to the west of High Street. However, the area is an integral part of the Lincoln City waterfront and an understanding of its development during the medieval period can play a key role in building up a picture of medieval suburban expansion and provide an insight into how the port and trade developed during the course of the medieval period.

Bibliography

Ash, L R ,and Orihel, T C, 1984 *Atlas of human parasitology*, 2nd edition, American Society of Clinical Pathologists Press, Chicago

Astill, G, and Grant, A, (eds) 1988 *The Countryside of Medieval England*, Oxford

Belshaw, R, 1989 A note on the recovery of Thoracochaeta zosterae (Haliday) (Diptera: Sphaeroceridae) from archaeological deposits, *Circaea*, **6**, 39-41

Binford, L, 1981 *Bones: ancient man and modern myth*, New York

Bond, J M, and O'Conner, T P, 1999 *Bones from Medieval Deposits at 16-22 Coppergate and other sites in York*, **15/5**, York Archaeology Trust/Council for British Archaeology

Brain, C K, 1981 *The Hunters or the hunted?* Chicago

Carrott, J, and Kenward, H K, 2001 Species associations amongst insect remains from urban archaeological deposits and their significance in reconstructing the past human environment, *J of Archaeol Science*, **28**, 887-905

Carver, M O H, 1979 Three Saxo-Norman tenements in Durham City, *Medieval Archaeol*, **23**, 1-80

Clapham, A, Tutin, T, and Moore, D, 1987 *Flora of the British Isles*, 3rd edition, Cambridge University Press

Cohen, A, and Serjeantson, D, 1996 *A manual for the identification of Bird Bones from Archaeological Sites*, London: Archetype Press

Colyer, C, 1975 Excavations at Lucy Tower Street, in Excavations at Lincoln 1970-1972: the western defences of the lower town; an interim report, *Antiq J*, **55**, 259-66

Connor, A, and Buckley, R, 1999 *Roman and Medieval Occupation in Causeway Lane, Leicester*, Leicester Archaeological Monog, **5**, Leicester University Press

Dainton, M, 1992 A quick, semi-quantitative method for recording nematode gut parasite eggs from archaeological deposits, *Circaea*, **9**, 58-63

Davey, P, 1971 Late Bronze Age metalwork from Lincolnshire, *Proceedings of the Prehistoric Society*, **37/1**, 96-111

Davey, P, 1973 Bronze Age metalwork from Lincolnshire, *Archaeologia*, **104**, 51-127

Davis, A, 1997 The plant remains, in C Thomas *et al* (eds) 1997, 234-245

Davis, A, 1999 Plant remains, in P Miller and R Stephenson 1999, 45-48

Deighton, K, 2001a Archive report on the animal bone from the excavation, in NA 2001

Deighton, K, 2001b Archive report on the shells from the excavation, in NA 2001

Dickson, C, and Dickson, J, 2000 *Plants and people in Ancient Scotland*, Tempus

Dobney, K M, Jaques, S D, and Irving, B G, 1994 *Of Butchers and Breeds. Report on vertebrate remains from various sites in the City of Lincoln*, Lincoln Archaeological Studies, **5**

Ellis, A E, 1969 *British Snails*, Clarendon Press, Oxford, reprint

Field, F N, 1986 An Iron Age timber causeway at Fiskerton, Lincolnshire, *Fenland Research*, **3**, 49-53

Fieller, N R J, Gilbertson, D D, and Ralph, N G A, (eds), 1985 *Palaeobiological investigations*, British Archaeol Reports, International Series, **266**, Oxford

Gale, R, and Cutler, D, 2000 *Plants in Archaeology*, Westbury and Royal Botanic Gardens, Kew

Godwin, H, 1956 *The History of the British Flora*, Cambridge

Greig, J, 1984 The palaeoecology of some British hay meadow types, in W Van Zeist and W A Casparie (eds) 1984 213-226

Greig, J, 1988 Plant resources, in G Astill and A Grant (eds), 1988, 108-27

Greig, J, 1991 The British Isles, in W van Zeist *et al* (eds) 1991, 229-334

Grieve, M, 1992 *A Modern Herbal*, Harmondsworth

Hall, A R, and Kenward, H K, 1980 An Interpretation of Biological Remains from Highgate, Beverley, *J of Archaeol Science*, **7**, 33-51

Hall, A R, and Kenward, H K, 1990 *Environmental Evidence from the Colonia, Tanner Row and Rougier Street*, The Archaeology of York, **14:6**, Council for British Archaeology, London

Halstead, P L, 1985 A study of mandibular teeth from Romano-British contexts at Maxey East, in F Pryor and C French 1985, 219-24

Irving, B, 1996 Fish, in K M Dobney *et al* 1996, 53-56

Jessop, L, 1986 Dung Beetles and Chafers, Coleoptera: Scarabaeoidea, *Handbooks for the Identification of British Insects* V, **11**, Royal Entomological Society of London

Jones, M J, and Jones, R H, 1981 Lincoln, in G Milne and B Hobley (eds) 1981, 138

Jones, M J, and Stocker, D, 2003 Settlement in the Lincoln area in the Prehistoric Era, in D Stocker (ed) 2003, 19-35

Kassai, T, 1998 *Veterinary helminthology*, Butterworth Heinemann

Kenward, H K, 1978 *The Analysis of Archaeological Insect Assemblages: a New Approach*, Archaeology of York, **19:1**, Council for British Archaeology/York Archaeological Trust

Kenward, H K, 1979 Five insect assemblages, in M O H Carver, 1979, 60- 67

Kenward, H K, 1997 Synanthropic Insects and the Size, Remoteness and Longevity of Archaeological Occupation sites: Applying Concepts from Biogeography to Past 'Islands' of Human Occupation, *Quaternary Proceedings*, **5**, 135-152

Kenward, H K, and Hall, A R, 1995 *Biological Evidence from Anglo-Scandinavian Deposits at 16-22 Coppergate*, The Archaeology of York, **14:7**, Council for British Archaeology, London

Kenward, H K, and Hall, A R, 1997 Enhancing Bio-Archaeological Interpretation Using Indicator Groups: Stable Manure as a Paradigm, *J of Archaeol Science*, **24**, 663-673

Kenward, H K, Hall, A R, and Jones, A K G, 1980 A Tested Set of Techniques for the Extraction of Plant and Animal Macrofossils from Waterlogged Archaeological Deposits, *Scientific Archaeol*, **22**, 3-15

Kerney, M P, and Cameron, R A D, 1979 *A Field Guide to the Snails of Britain and North-west Europe*, London

Lucht, W H, 1987 *Die Kafer Mitteleuropas*, Katalog, Krefeld

Mabey, R, 1996 *Flora Britannica*, Random House

Macan, T T, 1977 *A key to the British Fresh and Brackish water Gastropods*, Freshwater Biological Association

Miller, P, and Stephenson, R, 1999 *A 14th-century pottery site in Kingston upon Thames, Surrey, Excavations at 70-76 Eden Stree*, Museum of London Archaeology Service, Archaeol Studies Series, **1**

Milne, G, and Hobley, B, (eds) 1981 *Waterfront archaeology in Britain and Northern Europe*, Council for British Archaeology Research Report, **41**

Mitchell, A, 1974 *A Field Guide to the Trees of Britain and Northern Europe*, London

Moffett, L C, and Smith, D N, 1997 Insects and Plants from a Late Medieval Tenement in Stone, Staffordshire, *Circaea*, **12:2**, 157-175

Morgan, R A, 1982 Tree-ring studies in the Somerset Levels; the examination of modern hazel growth in Bradfield Woods, Suffolk, and its implications for the prehistoric data, *Ancient Monuments Laboratory Report*, **3839**

NA 2001 *Brayford North, Lincoln; post-excavation assessment and updated project design*, Northamptonshire Archaeology, unpublished client report

Osborne, P J, 1983 An Insect Fauna from a Modern Cesspit and its Comparison with Probable Cesspit Assemblages from Archaeological Sites, *J of Archaeol Science*, **10**, 453-463

Payne, S, 1973 Kill off patterns in sheep and goats: the mandibles from Asvan Kale, *Anatolian Studies*, **23**, 281-303

Payne, S, and Munson, P, 1985 Ruby and how many squirrels?, in N R J Fieller *et al* (eds), 1985, 31-40

Pryor, F, and French, C, 1985 *The Fenland Project No 1. Archaeology and environment in the Lower Welland Valley*, East Anglian Archaeol, **27 (i-ii)**

Pryor, F, 2001 *The Flag Fen Basin: archaeology and environment of a Fenland landscape*, London

Rackham, J, 2001 *Brayford North: the environmental assessment*, in NA 2001

Rackham, O, 1976 (1990 edition) *Trees and Woodland in the British Landscape*, Dent

Renfrew, C, (ed) 1991 *New Light on Early Farming. Recent Developments in Palaeoethnobotany*, Edinburgh

Robinson, M, and Wilson, R, 1983 *A survey of the environmental archaeology of the South Midlands*

Robson, J D, George, H, and Heaven, F W, 1974 *Soils in Lincolnshire I: Sheet TF 16 (Woodhall Spa)*, Harpenham, Soil Survey of England and Wales

Samuels, J, and Rosenberg, N, 2000 A *specification for Archaeological Excavation and Watching Brief at the Brayfield Centre, Lincoln*, unpublished John Samuels Archaeological Consultant Report

Schmid, E, 1972 *An atlas of animal bone*, London, Elsevier

Skidmore, P, 1999 The Diptera, in A Connor, and R Buckley 1999

Smith, D N, 1995 *Report on the insect remains from Winchester Palace, Southwark*, unpublished report for Museum of London Archaeology Service

Smith, D N, 1998 *The insect remains from Saxon and Medieval deposits at Bull Wharf, London*, unpublished report for Museum of London Archaeology Service

Smith, D N, 1999 *The insect remains from Preacher's Court, London*, The University of Birmingham Environmental Archaeology Services Report, **3**

Smith, D N, 2001 *The Insect Remains from One Poultry*, The University of Birmingham Environmental Archaeology Services Report, **13**

Smith, D N, and Chandler, G, 1995 *The insect remains from various features from the Priory of St. John's Clerkenwell*, unpublished report for Museum of London Archaeology Service

Smith, K G V, 1973 *Insects and Other Arthropods of Medical Importance*, British Museum (Natural History)

Smith, K G V, 1989 An introduction to the Immature Stages of British Flies, in *Handbooks for the identification of British Insects*, **10:14**, Royal Entomological Society of London, London

Steane, K, Darling, M J, Mann, J, Vince, A, and Young, J, 2001 *The Archaeology of Wigford and the Brayford Pool*, Lincoln Archaeological Studies, **2**, Oxbow Books

Stocker, D, (ed) 2003 *The City by the Pool: Assessing the archaeology of the city of Lincoln*, Lincoln Archaeological Studies, **10**, Oxbow Books

Taylor, E L, 1955 Parasitic helminths in medieval remains, *Veterinary Record*, **67**, 216

Taylor, M, 2001 Appendix 8, Archive report on the wood, in NA 2001

Thomas, C, Sloane, B, and Philpotts, C, (eds) 1997 *Excavations at the Priory and Hospital of St Mary Spital, London*, Museum of London Archaeology Service monog, **1**

Tutin, T G, Heywood, V H, Burges, N A, Valentine, D H, and Moore, D M, 1978-80 *Flora Europaea*, **1-5**, Cambridge University Press

van der Veen, M, 1991 Consumption or production? Agriculture in the Cambridgeshire Fens, in C Renfrew (ed) 1991, 349-361

Van Zeist, W, and Casparie, W A, (eds) 1984 *Plants and Ancient Man*, Rotterdam, Balkema

van Zeist, W, Wasylikowa, K, and Behre, K, (eds) 1991 *Progress in Old World Palaeoethnobotany*, Rotterdam

Vince, A, 1993 *A Tale of Two Cities: Lincoln and London compared*

Vince, A, 2003 The New Town: Lincoln in the High Medieval Era (*c* 900 to *c* 1350). A) The archaeological account, in D Stocker (ed) 2003, 159-302

Walker, D, 1970 Direction and rate in some British post-glacial hydroseres, in D Walker and R G West 1970

Walker, D, and West, R G, 1970 *Studies in vegetational history of the British Isles*, Cambridge University Press

White, A J, 1979 *Antiquities from the River Witham. Part 1 Prehistoric and Roman*, Lincolnshire Museums Information Sheet, Archaeological Series, **12**, Lincoln

Wilson, C A, 1991 *Food and drink in Britain*, London

www.ingramcontent.com/pod-product-compliance
Lightning Source LLC
Chambersburg PA
CBHW061303270326
41932CB00029B/3459